Lighting for Animation

The Art of Visual Storytelling

P. Jasmine Katatikarn and Michael Tanzillo

CRC Press
Taylor & Francis Group
Boca Raton London New York

CRC Press is an imprint of the
Taylor & Francis Group, an **informa** business

Still from the animated short *Mac and Cheese*. Property of Colorbleed Animation Studio.

Lighting for Animation is designed with one goal in mind—to make you a better artist. Over the course of the book, Jasmine Katatikarn and Michael Tanzillo (Senior Lighting TDs, Blue Sky Studios) will train your eye to analyze your work more critically, and teach you approaches and techniques to improve your craft. Focusing on the main philosophies and core concepts utilized by industry professionals, this book builds the foundation for a successful career as a lighting artist in visual effects and computer animation. Inside you'll find in-depth instruction on:

- Creating mood and storytelling through lighting
- Using light to create visual shaping
- Directing the viewer's eye with light and color
- Gathering and utilizing reference images
- Successfully lighting and rendering workflows
- Rendering layers and how they can be used most effectively
- Specific lighting scenarios, including character lighting, environment lighting, and lighting an animated sequence
- Material properties and their work with lighting
- Compositing techniques essential for a lighter
- A guide on how to start your career and achieve success as a lighting artist.

This book is not designed to teach software packages—there are websites, instructional manuals, online demos, and traditional courses available to teach you how to operate specific computer programs. That type of training will teach you how to create an image; this book will teach you the technical skills you need to make that image beautiful.

P. Jasmine Katatikarn is a Senior Lighting Technical Director at Blue Sky Studios. She holds a BA in Economics/Art History from Vassar College and received her Master of Science in Digital Imaging and Design degree from NYU. After graduate school, she began working in the field of 3D medical visualization and moved onto VFX/commercial work, working at The Mill, Framestore, and Rhinofx for seven years before moving into feature animated film work at Blue Sky Studios. Her lighting credits include *Peanuts*, *Rio 2*, *Epic*, *Ice Age: Continental Drift*, *Rio*, *Ice Age: Dawn of the Dinosaurs*, *Ghost Town*, and *The Nanny Diaries*.

Michael Tanzillo is a Senior Lighting Technical Director at Blue Sky Studios. He began his career as a photographer and studio artist after completing his BFA degree in Photography from Ohio State. Michael switched his career focus and freelanced as a 3D artist before attending the Savannah College of Art and Design and receiving his MFA in Visual Effects. In 2008, Michael joined the lighting team at Blue Sky Studios and his lighting credits include *Peanuts*, *Rio 2*, *Epic*, *Ice Age: Continental Drift*, *Rio*, *Scrat's Continental Crack-up* and *Ice Age: Dawn of the Dinosaurs*. Michael has also been credited as a compositing artist on multiple projects.

CRC Press
Taylor & Francis Group
6000 Broken Sound Parkway NW, Suite 300
Boca Raton, FL 33487-2742

First issued in hardback 2020

ISBN-13: 978-1-138-01866-2 (hbk)
ISBN-13: 978-1-138-01867-9 (pbk)
ISBN-13: 978-1-315-77959-1 (ebk)

Library of Congress Cataloging in Publication Data
Katatikarn, Jasmine.
Lighting for animation : the art of visual storytelling / Jasmine Katatikarn and Michael Tanzillo.
pages cm
ISBN 978-1-138-01867-9 (pbk.) — ISBN 978-1-138-01866-2 (hardback) — ISBN 978-1-315-77959-1 (ebook) 1. Computer animation. 2. Computer graphics. 3. Photography—Lighting. 4. Visual communication. I. Tanzillo, Michael. II. Title.
TR897.7.K385 2016
777'.7—dc23
2015020224

Typeset in Myriad Pro
Designed and typeset by Michelle Staples

Visit the Taylor & Francis Web site at
http://www.taylorandfrancis.com

and the CRC Press Web site at
http://www.crcpress.com

Contents

Special Acknowledgments

This book could not have been completed without the help and support of so many people. We want to thank all the artists and filmmakers who submitted the amazing work to help make this book more beautiful, including Housein Rodrigo Cornell (modeling) and Joshua Merck (rigging/animation) for their help bringing our LightBulb Family to life.

To our friends and family we want to say thank you for your unconditional support. Especially Vadim Turchin and Susan Tanzillo, whose contributions were essential to the successful completion of this project.

Jasmine & Mike

The Secret Life of Kells. Courtesy of Cartoon Saloon, Les Armateurs and Vivi Film.

Introduction

Lighting for Animation is designed with one goal in mind—to make you a better artist. Over the course of this book, we will strive to train your eye to analyze your work more critically by teaching you approaches and techniques that will enable you to improve your craft. We will focus on the main philosophies and core concepts utilized by industry professionals with the intention of building your foundation for a successful career as a lighting artist in visual effects and computer animation.

This book is not designed to teach specific software packages. There are websites, instructional manuals, online demos, and traditional courses available to teach you how to open a specific computer program and press all the right buttons. That type of training will teach you how to create an image; this book is designed to teach you how to make that image beautiful. We will teach you how to translate that technical skill into a successful and aesthetically polished final image.

The software package is just a tool. You are the artist. To use a metaphor, we don't want to just teach you how to use a hammer; we want to train you to be a carpenter. We want you to have the type of training that will allow you to think critically and problem-solve intelligently to tackle any situation. After all, software comes and goes. Studios will have customized workflows or proprietary, in-house software. So learning a specific package does not necessarily translate to a better working knowledge once in the industry. Rest assured that the knowledge you gain from *Lighting for Animation* will be applicable to your work regardless of where your career leads.

At the end of the day, studios are looking for a good artistic eye and the skill to execute a successful final image. They understand new employees will need to be trained in their proprietary practices and software, but what they cannot train is your ability to see, analyze, and make the proper adjustments to produce a complete and polished shot. These are the elements that *Lighting for Animation* will put at the forefront to help you reach your full potential.

When done well, lighting can bring beauty and magic to a shot. © Disney.

1

Why we Light

Animated films are born when skilled and passionate artists merge their talents to build a story within a universe of extraordinary possibilities. Designers dream up the world, modelers build the world, riggers give the world the ability to move, and animators make the world sing and dance. It is the job of the lighter to make that world beautiful; to give it shape and life and an unmistakable soul. Lighting is about taking geometry and transforming it to create a setting the audience can submerse themselves into, thus allowing the film to take them on a journey. Ultimately, like all departments in an animation studio, the lighter's goal is to tell a story.

The Role of Lighting

Lighting for animation is an art unto itself, and a subtle one at that. When viewing an animated work the contributions made by other artists are clear. The audience can see all the props in the scene and know a modeler must have constructed objects in 3D space. The characters' movements are evidence of the animator's work. Lighting, like a musical score, works on a rooted, more psychological level. Lighting does not necessarily stand out as an element in the scene but is more *felt* by the audience. The audience generally does not identify each individual light or even pay much attention to what time of day is being portrayed. Instead, viewers *feel* lighting's influence and react to it subconsciously.

A lighter on an animated film has three main goals in mind. These goals will be discussed in detail over the course of this book but they will be introduced now. The first goal is to direct the viewer's eye. The lighter will use luminance, contrast, color, and any other means necessary to craft the scene in a way for the audience to focus on the action. Scenes can become incredibly complex and it is the lighter's job to ensure that the audience is focusing on the area of the screen that is most important to the story. This is also critical when a shot is very short and the audience has limited time to focus on the main story point of the shot.

The second goal is to create visual interest in the scene by defining good shaping in all objects. Visual shaping in computer graphics (CG) is similar to painting in that the artist is creating value differences so the two-dimensional objects on the flat screen can be perceived as existing in three-dimensional space. By creating light,

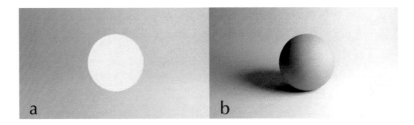

Figure 1.1 Both of these images are the same geometry. The visual shaping caused by creating a variety of tones using light and shadow gives the sphere in Image B more volume, weight, and visual interest.

color, or value variations across an object to give it more volume, an artist can make CG objects appear more visually interesting.

The third major responsibility of the lighter is to help tell the story by establishing the mood. Again, all artists on an animated project are working toward telling a single story and it is essential that every facet of the film strives to tell the best story possible. The story notes a lighter may receive are often based on creating a specific emotion such as:

- Make this shot more romantic.
- The audience needs to feel this character's sinister motives.
- Tension needs to build over the course of these three shots.

There are many tools that a lighter has at his or her disposal to help set the mood. One major tool is the use of color design. Through the use of color and light, a lighter can influence the viewer's subconscious reaction when first viewing the scene. In Figure 1.2, the set and camera angle are nearly identical in each shot but notice how the mood changes significantly depending on the light and color values.

Figure 1.2 Whether it is the crisp, clean daylight, the warm orange glow of the evening's "magic hour", or the cooler evening lighting, the color palette greatly influences the mood of each of these shots. Stills from the animated short *The Fantastic Flying Books of Mr. Morris Lessmore*. Property of Moonbot Studios.

Color is also used extremely effectively to set the mood in this scene from *Edmond était un âne (Edmond Was A Donkey)* in Figure 1.3 In this shot, Edmond is unhappy and dreary about life. The lighting was designed with cool blues to instantly portray a feeling of sadness and melancholy. As the shot progresses, warm light enters from offscreen creating a feeling of optimism and hope. This feeling is not communicated through dialog or actions but instead with a simple color design consisting of warm and cool light.

Figure 1.3 The introduction of warm light completely alters the mood of this otherwise cool-toned shot. Stills from the animated short *Edmond était un âne (Edmond was a Donkey)*. Property of Papy3d/ONF NFB/ARTE.

diffusion

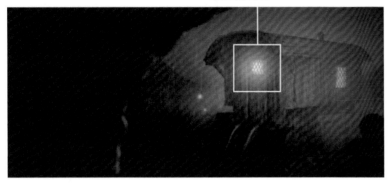

Figure 1.4 Diffusion in this shot was added around the window and other light sources. Still from the animated short *Little Freak*. Property of Edwin Schaap.

Figure 1.5 Diffusion has been used since silent era Hollywood films.

Diffusion is another visual element that helps set the mood of the shot. When artists speak of diffusion they are referring to the effects of a soft light source causing glow and blur over the entire image, giving it a sense of magic. Increasing diffusion is accomplished by evenly spreading the light from a light source creating a softer feel as seen in Figure 1.4.

This concept of using soft light to give the image a glow is a tried and proven film technique. During the era of early cinema, adding practical elements like petroleum jelly to the lens to achieve the same look was common practice. This softness is once again something that is not necessarily recognized by the audience, but is definitely felt and used to influence the audience's mood. Present-day animated films simply picked up on this already established aesthetic and implemented it.

The soft and diffused look is an excellent example of lighting playing a psychological role in the telling of the story in a similar way to a musical score. The musical equivalent would be a romantic tune that is soothing to keep the audience engaged. The music would flow evenly and effortlessly without abrupt changes that could startle the audience.

Drama and horror films have much heavier, deeper notes to help audibly set the mood. There are quick changes and jumps in the music that could put the audience on edge. The visual equivalent is a dark and high contrast image to convey an evil theme. This type of look goes back to the earliest days of cinema as similar techniques were displayed in one of the first and most influential of early horror films, *Nosferatu*. In this movie, the contrast is extremely dramatic and many sections of the frame fall into complete darkness while other sections illuminate past the point that the film can record, creating a white, "blown-out" look.

Without the use of effective lighting, movies would fall short of telling a complete story to the viewers. To successfully bring the emotions and story of a film to the audience, every artist from the previsualization stages through lighting must work together with one task in mind: to tell a story.

Creating Visual Shaping

At its core, visual shaping is a way of giving objects in a two-dimensional image a sense of height, depth, weight, and volume. Take, for example, a simple cube. A cube is a known object that has six sides. If positioned and lit in a certain way, the cube will communicate to the audience as a flat plane, lacking depth and dimension (Figure 1.7a). Even if the cube is positioned properly, the lighting can cause the cube to look flat, depriving the audience of the proper understanding of the space and shape of the object (Figure 1.7b). Therefore, if nothing else, the goal of visual shaping within lighting is to communicate this shape and volume to the audience (Figure 1.7c).

By lighting a scene with good visual shaping, the lighter has the power to bring more depth and the feeling of complexity to a shot that would otherwise fall, quite literally, flat.

Figure 1.6 *Nosferatu* is a classic film that uses dark shadows and high contrast to add to the suspenseful mood. *Nosferatu* (1922), Jofa–Atelier Berlin–Johannisthal, Prana–Film GmbH.

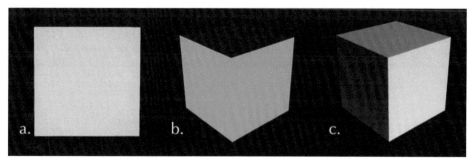

Figure 1.7 The same cube can be portrayed in different ways by changing the position and lighting.

Figure 1.8 In this shot, the position and intensity of the sunlight draws the viewer's eye toward the character and the mural on the wall. © Disney.

Directing the Viewer's Eye

Another lighting technique that influences the story is something so basic and simple that it is often overlooked. The lighter needs to answer the question, "What part of the image should be the audience's focus?" Shots can be a few seconds or fewer in length and it is absolutely crucial for the audience to know exactly where to look in order to read the action of a shot.

Lighters can use light, contrast, color, or any means possible to direct the audience's eye. Generally speaking, the viewer's eyes are drawn to the brightest object on the screen. This bright part of the screen can be accentuated even more if surrounded by darker values. In the examples in Figure 1.9, the eye immediately focuses on the main character and the other areas of the shots become secondary. This is commonly referred to as being "light over dark."

This can also work in reverse. A darker character can be placed in front of a lighter background and that high contrast can draw the viewer's eye. Looking at the frame below from *The Fantastic Flying Books of Mr. Morris Lessmore*, the eye is immediately drawn to the bright window and then settles on the contrast of the darker character, making that character the central focus. Specifically, the focus is on the character's head so the audience will be more inclined to watch his eyes and help read his emotions.

Figures 1.9a Concept Art from *Song of the Sea*—Courtesy of Cartoon Saloon, Melusine Productions, The Big Farm, Superprod, Norlum.

1.9b Still from the animated short *The Fantastic Flying Books of Mr. Morris Lessmore*. Property of Moonbot Studios.

Contrasting colors is another method lighters use to make elements of an image stand out. Take these colored squares in Figure 1.10b, for example. Notice how the center square draws the audience's eye immediately. Whether it is light vs. dark, warm vs. cool, or the use of complementary colors, these are all viable options when trying to direct the viewer's eye.

Figure 1.10a A good example of the use of complementary red suits over green foliage making the characters really pop out on screen. © Disney.

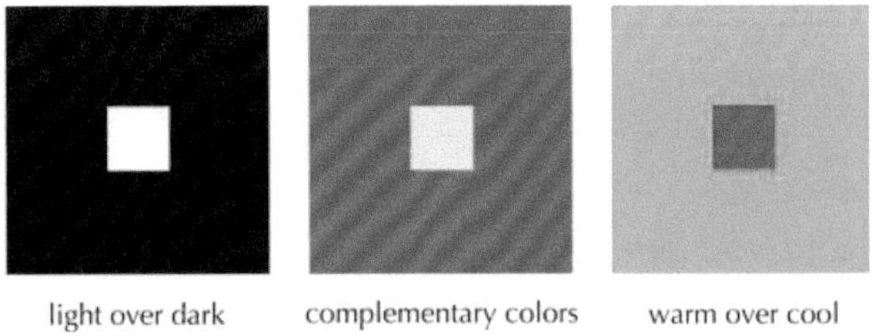

light over dark   complementary colors   warm over cool

Figure 1.10b These squares demonstrate how the use of colors and values can make an object stand out on the screen.

Final Thoughts

If a shot has set the proper mood, created good visual shaping, and directed the viewer's eye, chances are it will be successful. These core elements are what are at the heart of lighting. This book will work to show you all the ins and outs of lighting, but each and every element relates back to at least one of these concepts. When these core concepts are followed, lighting can move the audience's spirit and enable them to connect with the film and allow the story to touch their souls.

Interview
with Chris Wedge

Creative Director and Co-Founder :: Blue Sky Studios.

Q. What is your current job/role at your company?
A. I am the Creative Director and Co-Founder of Blue Sky Studios.

Q. How did you get started in this industry?
A. I got started very early in computer animation. I had done stop-motion animation as a kid and in college. I loved making a little set look big by using camera position and lights. It was one thing to look at the miniature in a room and another thing entirely to look at it through the camera. Through the camera it became another world entirely. I learned about a lot about lighting for films by lighting those little sets.

I became interested in 3D animation because it had a lot of the same qualities as stop-motion. It was fun to transform geometry into another world. The dimensional nature of the 3D world was fantastic and I began working in it back around 1980. I was actually one of the first animators ever to use 3D animation.

Q. Any non-CG artwork that inspires you?
A. It's all about the project. There is an aesthetic you bring to any particular project and I feel that the aesthetic needs to focus the spectrum of emotion. Sometimes it's painting, sometimes it's photography. When we were working on *Epic*, we looked at a lot of N.C. Wyeth. He did beautiful renderings for classic story illustration. Very romantic, very complete artwork. Sculptural paintings of natural environments with classic compositions and a beautiful palette. When you look at those images you get a lot of dimension and romanticism and that was one artist that inspired me during *Epic*.

Q. If you could tell yourself one thing when first starting in this industry, what would it be?

A. Follow your heart. If you feel passionately about something just continue with it and do the work you believe in. Do not let people talk you out of ideas if you truly believe it is best. It's different for everyone, and of course you will always deal with compromise, but more often than not your instincts are right. I've always been most successful when I was true to my own instincts. When you apply the advice of too many people the message can get blurred.

That being said, you want to listen to those around you because you never know where the next good idea is going to come from. Be open to advice, but choose wisely whether or not you act upon that advice. Listen to criticism—especially when it is consistent. I grew up not trusting anyone, like a lot of people in my generation. As I've grown older, I've realized that sometimes they know what they are talking about.

Q. Is there any one sequence or project from your career that stands out to you?

A. Hopefully there are a bunch of them!

Specifically the one that stands out is the cave painting sequence in *Ice Age*. It is the moment that Manny's back story is explored and presented to the audience. I felt that scene gave the film the depth of emotion that allowed the audience to invest further than just the comedy and really connect to the characters. That was a special sequence.

In *Epic*, I enjoyed the sequences that allowed us to go in and explore that magical world. It was particularly great to go into the battle sequence on a lily pond with these tiny people and make it look kinetic, dangerous, and full of action. That sequence exemplified the type of life and energy I wanted to bring to that world. That was a lot of fun.

Q. What is lighting's largest contribution to an animated film?

A. Lighting controls a certain spectrum of the story that is just as important as the acting, the quality of the motion, the dialogue, or the music. It's part of how we focus perspective and it creates the mood with associations we make. It's what we use to control the audience's experience and determine what they are looking at.

Every film is coded with subconscious color palettes and a range of emotional dialogue that is controlled with composition, lighting, and music. Different aspects of the story get different colors, saturation values, and contrast levels. It's important to establish that palette and keep it consistent throughout the film.

Good guys and bad guys get contrasting elements. In *Epic*, there was a battle in the forest and the contradicting colors were the verdant greens and deep forest colors of the heroes versus the evil characters which looked more like bare bark, gray rock, and black fungus.

Spring-like greens and colors that represent life in the forest were allocated to the good guys and the evil guys were desaturated and cooler, to represent the death of the forest. All non-fantastical characters like the humans fell in between with more salmon-like colors that were desaturated and muted just a bit to distinguish them from the fantasy characters. These types of color distinctions, which are aided by the lighting, are crucial to the film.

Q. After being in this industry for over thirty years, has your approach toward lighting changed?
A. At Blue Sky, we started because of lighting. We started the company with the goal of making images that no one had ever seen before. That was twenty-seven years ago. When we started out, we were geeks about raytracing technology. We knew that if we had enough computing power and time, we could make images that were indistinguishable from photographs. We never thought of that as the finish line, but if we had the power to do that, we could do anything with CG. Back then, raytracing was only done in labs and had not been applied to anything with commercial viability. So for us, it has always been about creating the subtleties of objects and interacting light and bringing that to an audience.

My first Blue Sky film was *Bunny* and that film took eight years to make. It was all about getting the technology to the point where I could tell a story that was dreamy and weird and convincing and complete. By today's standards it is a little rough around the edges, but it definitely has its moments. For me and Carl Ludwig, it was all about creating the complexities that convince us something is real. Lighting is an incredible thing and we take it for granted in our daily lives.

As far as developing over time, lighting is completely project driven. In the past decade or so, it hasn't been about achieving technical goals, but telling stories with the most impact. We are at the point now where duplicating the real world or photography isn't the goal. It is about using the technology to create an aesthetic to tell the story. This is truly an exciting time to work in this industry.

Runaway (September 20, 1958), Norman Rockwell. Reference image from *Norman Rockwell: Behind the Camera*.
Printed by permission of the Norman Rockwell Family Agency. Copyright © The Norman Rockwell Family Entities.

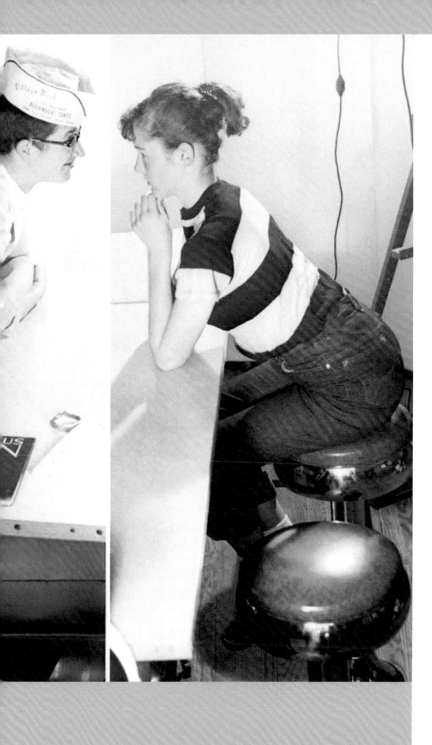

2

Observing the World Around Us

Reference is an essential part of any artist's workflow. Whether painting, sculpting, or working in 3D on a computer, an artist must study the world in order to replicate it. Whether an artist is sketching based on observations from a live model or painting shadows after breaking down a photographic image, reference is a tool utilized by artists of all disciplines.

How and why do we use reference? What are the consequences when we do not use reference? What are some methods of evaluating reference and translating that into a visual image? What are the best techniques for gathering and organizing reference? This chapter will explore and answer these questions.

The Importance of Reference

Memory is a funny thing. The way people will think something looks can be vastly different from reality. Human beings often fabricate qualities about an object that are not actually there. Sometimes they fabricate the existence of objects altogether. Shapes, colors, and scale can all be skewed by what researchers call "false memories."

False memory was researched in the study, "Decreased false memory for visually presented shapes and symbols among adults on the autism spectrum" by Ashleigh Hillier, Heather Campbell, Jocelyn Keillor, Nicole Phillips, and David Q. Beversdorf, published in the *Journal of Clinical and Experimental Neuropsychology* (2007). In that study, twenty-three young adults with no history of mental impairment were shown twenty-four sets of twelve slide projections. The slides consisted of different geometric shapes, which varied in size, position, shape, color, and number. After viewing each set of slides, the participants were shown five additional slides and asked if each of the five additional slides were in the original set. Of the additional five cards, two were from the original set, two were obviously different cards containing shapes not found in any of the originals, and the last card was called the "Lure." The "Lure" was similar to the original set in many ways, but not identical to any of the originals.

In 80 percent of the trials, participants were able to accurately identify the images they had seen in the original. The participants were nearly perfect at picking out the two distinctly different images, with a success rate of 98 percent. The "Lure" image, however, was falsely identified in a staggering 60 percent of the trials. This was referred to by Dan Schachter at Harvard as 'gist' memory. People generally do not remember every detail but rather the gist of things, which makes it challenging when attempting to accurately recreate images simply from memory.

Let us test this out. Close your eyes and think about the room you are currently in. Think of the color of the ceiling. Now, lift your head toward the ceiling and open your eyes and take a look. Really look. Do not just think what the paint color is: actually look at the

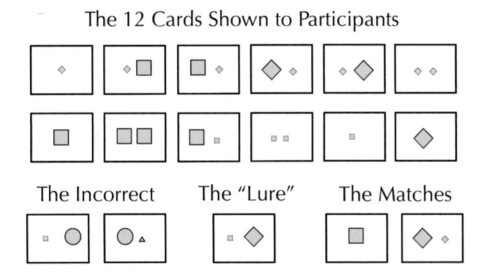

Figure 2.1 The top twelve images represent the cards shown to the subjects of the study. The bottom five were the cards the subjects were asked to match to the original group. The "Lure" was misidentified as being in the original group 60 percent of the time.

colors as they exist in front of you. Even if the ceiling is painted white, it may appear more gray than white if not illuminated. The lights in the room may be casting a color or there may be some colors bleeding onto the ceiling from the surrounding colored walls.

An individual would not usually be able to pick up on every detail in the room by pure memory alone. Normally, there are just too many objects and details to remember. This is where analyzing reference helps the artist correctly recall elements of the world. Human beings are much better at distinguishing specific characteristics of an object, like color and brightness, with much more accuracy when using a visual example and not simply by relying on their memory. In fact, there are times when our mind will actually fill in gaps of our memories with false, fabricated information that we believe to be true.

Research has shown that while the eye can perceive objects as thousands of different colors, the brain tries to categorize everything into about eleven different color categories. Things are blue, red, black, white, etc. People often remember tomatoes as pure red, lemons as yellow, and eggplants as purple when in reality the actual color of those objects can be much more diverse. The human mind simply distorts our memory of a given object so it more neatly falls into one of those verbal categories.

Therefore, it is vital to have an actual visual representation of an object as reference. Whether it is a photograph, sculpture, painting, or the object itself, it must be something tangible that the artist can compare against when creating. Relying solely on the mind's eye will lead to inaccurate and ultimately less successful results.

What Happens When an Artist Does Not Use Reference?

Simply put, ignoring reference will lead to an inefficient workflow and a final image that is less successful. Reference gives the artist a visual goal and a blueprint for constructing the image. Without it, the result may look different from that intended and the artist will have no idea why. With reference one can compare the images and determine that, in fact, an area needs to be brighter or perhaps the shadow area needs a bit more color for it to be read more naturally.

Additionally, lighting artists are rarely working on projects alone. Generally there are teams of artists that work on a sequence of shots simultaneously and coordinate the look. One artist's shots will cut with all the others and the objects in the scene must appear the same to maintain consistency. Reference is essential in these instances since it allows the team to collectively assemble their ideas and focus the goals on a specific look.

Some might think reference is unnecessary since the animated project consists of an imaginary character or world. This is absolutely not the case. Reference plays as large a role in animated projects with imaginary characters as lighting a human to be seamlessly and photorealistically inserted into a background plate. The one thing to keep in mind is that, although the characters are unique, all of their individual elements can be based on real life objects as components.

An imaginary character like Shrek is a great example of this. There are no ogres found in nature but artists often reference

human characteristics so the audience can more easily form a connection with the character. In fact, some people believe the artists who designed Shrek referenced one particular human named Maurice Tillet. Tillet was a professional wrestler during the 1930s to the 1950s but was also a scholar who wrote poetry and spoke fourteen different languages. He suffered from a medical condition called *Acromegaly* which caused his bones to grow uncontrollably. Whether or not he was the basis for Shrek, we can begin to get an understanding of how an artist can use real world characteristics to help design fantastical characters.

Figure 2.2 Some speculate the design of *Shrek* was based on a French wrestler named Maurice Tillet. (left) Shrek © 2004 Dream Works Animation LLC. All rights reserved. (right) Copyright Associated Press.

Gathering Reference

All artists should be gathering reference from a variety of sources. Reference can be found in actual physical objects, photography, fine arts (such as paintings and drawings), and in films and television.

Photography

Photography is a very common source of reference and is very easy to find. The best reference photographs are not highly processed or adjusted. Using photographs, one can easily pinpoint and analyze the variations and distinctions of different lighting scenarios. The artist can view elements like color, value, contrast, and many other aspects of an image that will need to be simulated in the scenes. The artist can also get a better understanding of how the colors appear differently in the same landscape depending on both changes in the time of day and changes in the season. This is a great way of breaking down specific exterior scenes to gain a full knowledge of that environment's characteristics.

Figure 2.3 The same environment can change drastically depending on the time of day. Photography is a great way to capture these variations in light color and quality (bottom row of images). Time of year also greatly influences the color and look of a scene and should be accounted for when lighting an animated project (top row of images).

Figure 2.4 The illumination of a man-made object like a television can be difficult to replicate in the render without good reference imagery to hit all the subtleties.

Figure 2.5 Reference also helps answer questions about light quality like "How much light escapes under and around the door of an illuminated room?" And, "What type of shadow does that lighting scenario create?"

Internal shots, like exterior shots, require just as much observation to obtain the knowledge of their unique lighting characteristics. We often overlook how light actually interacts around us, but as a lighter we need to observe these effects in order to be able to reproduce them accurately in our computer generated worlds. Using the example mentioned previously in this chapter, we need to closely observe the color of the ceiling before we can accurately reproduce it.

Another example is how interiors are lit in specific lighting circumstances. In the examples in Figures 2.4 and 2.5, we ask the question, "How does the room look when the only source of illumination is the TV?" Or, "How much light actually spills under the door while someone is lying in bed at night? What types of shadows does this light create?"

Interior lighting setups are common in everyday lives but contain subtleties that can often go overlooked. Let's take a closer look at Figure 2.5. What observations can be made by looking at this image?

The first step is to identify where the main light source is coming from. In this instance, it is coming from behind the cracked door (marked in orange). There is a nice glow effect on the door that comes from the light within (purple). The shadows that are formed from the light create an interesting shape along the floor and the wall, something that may not have been expected if one did not see it in the reference (blue). The light from the door is reflecting on the floor and against the wall on the right side (magenta). This tells the observer something about the reflective properties of the floor and wall. Look closer and one can see that the wall's reflection is softer than the floor's reflection. These are just a few observations that can be pulled from this reference image.

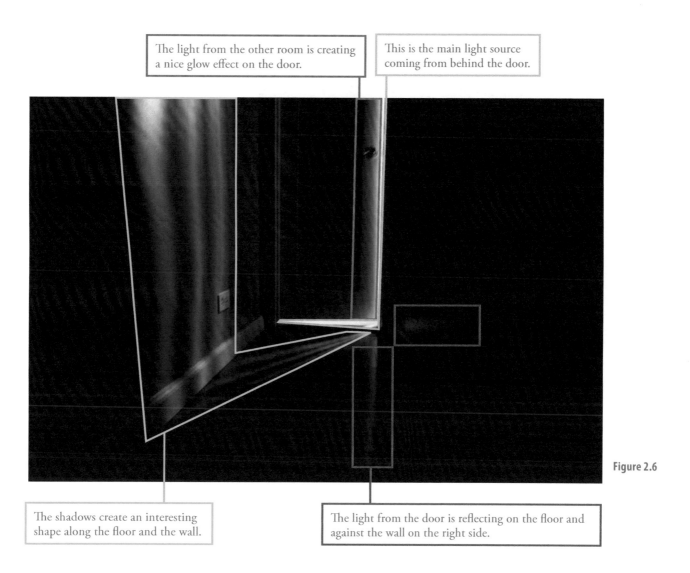

The light from the other room is creating a nice glow effect on the door.

This is the main light source coming from behind the door.

The shadows create an interesting shape along the floor and the wall.

The light from the door is reflecting on the floor and against the wall on the right side.

Figure 2.6

Obtaining reference images that help hone in on the lighting details of a shot will result in more successful and believable images. The reference image does not even need to be relevant at the time. If it strikes the artist as something interesting and engaging, he or she should capture that moment and save it for later. Good reference photographs always find a way to be applicable at some point.

Figure 2.7 Albert Bierstadt's *The Trappers' Camp* is an fantastic example of lighting that is a mixture of natural light with the man-made campfire light. *The Trappers' Camp* (1861), Albert Bierstadt, Yale University Art Gallery, Hartford, Connecticut.

Fine Arts

Traditional media, like sculpture or painting, often get overlooked when CG artists are searching for reference. This is a mistake because much can be learned by analyzing these more traditional forms of art. Paintings are particularly useful to lighters since the conceptual approach is much the same for both artists. Both will sculpt light into a space independent of the physics of nature. A photographer works with real world calculations and limitations while a painter is free to bend the laws of physics in order to create whatever image he or she wishes. One just needs to maintain some level of believability to the audience; 3D artists have that same flexibility.

Albert Bierstadt's *The Trappers' Camp* (Figure 2.7) is a fantastic example of a painting whose lighting can be broken down and referenced for a CG scene. Look at the mixture of natural light with the man-made campfire light. The color contrast between the two is dramatic and could definitely be something that might be referenced for the light color, light intensity, and shadow values in a 3D scene, even though it may not be scientifically accurate.

Television, Film, and Video Reference

Television, film, and video are potentially the best source of reference because they are the closest thing to an animated project's final product. There are normally moving characters, sets, and cameras in animated shots so this animated reference is extremely beneficial. One can observe how a character looks as they travel between light and shadow or how the ground shadow changes as the wind blows the trees.

Lighting for an animated film also requires the use of lights with animated values like a flickering candle or a camera's flash bulb that can only be referenced by television, film, or footage shot by the artist. How fast does an automobile's headlight pass a stationary object? At what speed does a neon sign click on and off? The timing and movement of these types of lights can be difficult to replicate without the use of video reference.

Animated films often mimic looks that have been established in television and film. Aesthetics like depth of field, lens flares, vignetting, film grain and lens distortions are all looks that were born in film-based media and incorporated into the look of an animated film. These aesthetics can be observed and analyzed in order to create a believable CG image.

Figure 2.8 *Out of the Past.* © mptvimages.com.

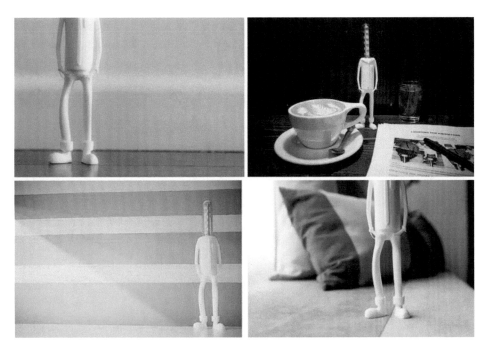

Figure 2.9 Ideally, artists would always have the actual object they are referencing to take into different lighting scenarios to get the most accurate reference possible.

Actual, Physical Reference

In a perfect world, an artist would have physical models to reference in every situation. That way the object could sit next to the artist at his or her workstation and could be accessible whenever analysis was required. One could observe how the object reacts and looks in different light settings to obtain valuable information on how light reacts directly and indirectly with the object.

Figure 2.9 is an example of how an artist would use an actual physical object to simulate the character in different environments for lighting reference. Even though the character is imaginary, he has been 3D printed to scale to study exactly how he would look in certain instances. The artist would take this object into lighting sce-narios that are specific to the animated project and photograph it for reference.

Unfortunately, access to physical reference is not always possible. If someone is looking for reference on how Paris looked in 1917 or how a sunset looks on Mars, physical reference is unattainable. Luckily, this is a unique time in history. Thanks to the Internet, never before has this wealth of information been as readily available as it is today. This information is not only in the form of facts and written words but in images as well. With a quick search, an artist can find images of practically anything and everything without leaving his or her seat. These images, along with ones created by the artist, will make up the bulk of the images in reference libraries.

Processing Reference

So what is an artist looking for when evaluating a reference image? Each situation is different but the general idea is to identify the characteristics that make a specific object, light, or character unique in a lighting scenario. An artist will also look for elements of a reference image that make the object feel more robust and visually appealing. Commonly observed characteristics are light direction, light intensity, color of light, shadow, and falloff.

Light Direction

For a lighter, one of the first characteristics analyzed is light direction. Where are the main light sources in the scene situated? The main indicators the artist wants to analyze are illumination, specular highlight, and shadow direction. By looking at these three indicators, the artist is almost always able to identify the position and direction of the main light sources on an object.

Light Intensity

Light intensity incorporates both the intensity of an individual light and the value relationship between that light and others. It also takes direct light and indirect light into account. Direct light consists of the primary light rays being cast by a light source. Indirect lighting is when those primary rays hit an object and refract off, influencing the surrounding areas.

Analyzing direct vs. indirect lighting is often referred to as the key to fill ratio. The key light is the main light source of any scene. Often it is the sun or moonlight but it can certainly be any artificial or man-made light as well. The fill value, in this instance, is the amount of light that is filling in the shadow cast by the key light. This fill value is made up of things like illumination from the sky and light bouncing off a surrounding wall and spilling onto the scene. Understanding the key to fill ratio helps understand the overall contrast level of the reference itself.

Figure 2.10 One analysis an artist must look into when reading reference is the key to fill ratio. The more fill light in a scene, the less the difference between the parts of the image illuminated by the key light and the parts illuminated by only the fill. More fill light means less contrast.

Color of Light

The color of light is a very important factor when scrutinizing reference images. Understanding the color from the key light is a fairly straightforward concept. An artist can analyze the specific light source in the image by data picking the area in an image editing software to help identify the specific color of that light source. Of course, light can change in the environment so it is important that this color be used as a starting point. The artist must remain flexible to adjust the colors in the scene if the result is undesirable.

From there it is a matter of matching the intensity and constantly comparing the created image with the original reference until they become aligned. This can be a very difficult task at first, but as an artist becomes more experienced, it gets easier.

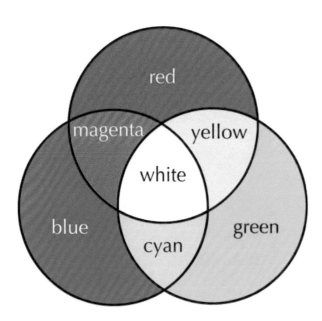

Figure 2.11a In order to fully understand the color of light, we must realize that light is an additive process that behaves differently from mixing paint. The color wheel of how red, green, and blue light colors mix together to form secondary colors.

Figure 2.11b A 3D scene with only one red, one green, and one blue light. Areas of yellow, cyan, and magenta are formed when those light colors mix.

indirect light color   direct light color

Figure 2.12 A light source like a tungsten bulb can have a very strong, warm tone that can be sampled in reference photographs and replicated in your own light.

Analyzing the secondary and indirect lights is more difficult. They are not as obvious but their proper application is necessary for the success of the image. Secondary lights can come from a multitude of sources. A secondary light can be the sky surrounding an environment casting a cool blue into the shadows on a bright sunny day. It can be a distant lamp or light source that is only slightly illuminating the scene.

These lights can also be indirect and caused by the key light hitting an object and reflecting light rays back onto the scene. A good example of this is a white object sitting atop a colored surface. The color of that surface bounces back up onto the white object and shows some "color bleed." This is an example of a bounce light, which is one type of secondary light. Bounce light and other secondary lights will be discussed in greater detail in Chapter 3.

For now, remember to question the influence of secondary light when analyzing reference by asking questions like,

- Does the green grass reflect the sunlight back up onto the character?
- Does the water create a caustic pattern on the underside of that bridge?

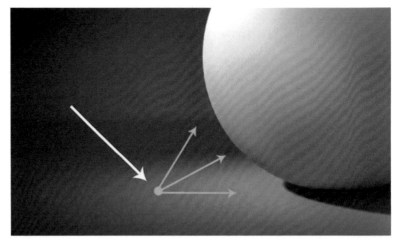

Figure 2.13 Indirect light and secondary light are when your primary, key light hits one surface and bounces off onto another. In this image, it can be seen how the bounce light color has changed depending on the color of the ground plane.

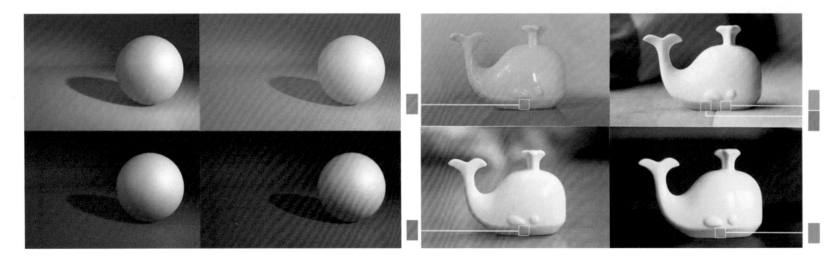

Figure 2.14 The same object photographed in different scenarios can pick up indirect, secondary light rays and absorb the color of surrounding objects.

Shadows

Shadows are an interesting trait to be investigated when looking at reference as well. Shadow color, softness, and shape are all elements that must be replicated in order for the entirety of the shot to work. By observing the shadow an artist can learn about not only the light direction, as previously stated, but also some characteristics of that light source. If it is a sharp, hard shadow, the light source is most likely relatively small in comparison to the object and/or far away, similar to a sun. If the shadow is soft, the artist knows the light source is more diffused, less direct, and possibly relatively large compared to the object being lit. In which direction are the shadows going? Are they drawn out along the ground or are they just beneath the character? This will give the artist an idea of the position at which the light source should be placed. Drawn out shadows will be the result of a light source coming from a lower angle than one that casts a shorter shadow.

Shadow color is something that is often overlooked. So often shadows are depicted as black with no variation or color, but if someone really looks at shadow references it will be observed that this is not the case. There are a multitude of variables that go into the color of a shadow. For example, does the blue sky give the shadows a tint of color? Is there light reflecting off surrounding objects and casting light into the shadows? When analyzing reference of a shadow, really look and think about what may be contributing to the color.

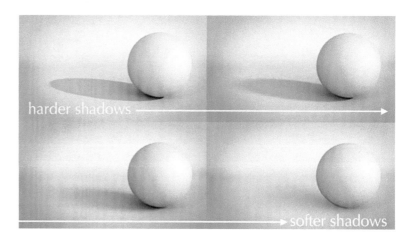

Figure 2.15 Shadow softness is determined by the light source. The larger the light source relative to the object being lit, the softer the shadow.

actual shadow color vs. plain black

Figure 2.16 Shadow color is incredibly important when trying to match to reference. Color picking certain areas so the shadow color is accurate is essential when trying to craft your image.

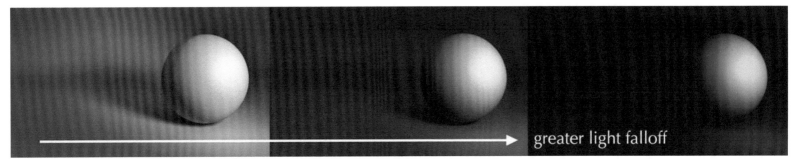

Figure 2.17

greater light falloff

natural fall off of a light

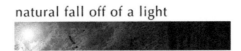

Figure 2.18 In this example, the light source starts off very strong and intense, but fades quickly in the surrounding trees before almost dying completely when it reaches the buildings.

Light Decay

All light sources, no matter what they are, have a finite distance they illuminate. Flashlights have the small beam of light that shoots out of the canister and travels only a certain distance. Candlelight can often decrease very quickly and shines light only on a very small area. Even the sun's light eventually dwindles in the vastness of space.

When lighting, it is important to also match the look of this falloff whenever it is necessary. Does an illuminated streetlight at dusk influence the lighting of a character walking at street level? Does the candle on one table affect the lighting of the characters sitting at the table next to it? Finding reference to the specific image an artist is trying to build and sticking to it will lead to the scene feeling more believable to the audience and ultimately lead to a better final product.

Utilizing Reference

Reference can be used in a couple of different ways. The first is to read the reference literally. An artist can try to match the reference exactly in terms of color, contrast, brightness, etc. This is especially likely when creating imagery that is meant to be either photoreal or matching a specific traditional artistic style like a painting or drawing. In these cases, a one-to-one match with the reference is ideal.

In other cases, it can be used when the artist is trying to create a look that is completely original. In these cases the artist will use the reference as a jumping-off point. The artist can pick only a certain element from the reference that suits the specific need but modify it in a way that allows it to drift away from the reference and into an entirely new, unique experience. Perhaps the colorcast from the night sky in a particular painting has caught the artist's eye, but the saturation could be pushed even further. The color of the sky would be referenced as the starting point and then enhanced for the final image.

Organizing Reference

The final step of gathering reference is organizing it into a library. This library will be useful to both the individual that created it and any other artists collaborating on the project. This is a common-sense idea, but is often overlooked by many artists who find the practice laborious and time consuming. Ultimately, using a reference library will save time and headaches as an individual continues to grow and develop as an artist.

Creating a functioning, useful library will ensure that the work put forth can best be used in the future. This library should be categorized and labeled with a common naming convention so a large number of images can be searched and managed simply.

There are many ways to create a reference library. One way is to create a file directory structure in a folder location, either on your computer, network, or online image database that is accessible to the necessary artists. Within the directory, create the categories and subfolders for the library. This should be done with some care as images will fall into multiple categories and either must be copied into each category, or tags of metadata must be created to enable all the other artists to search the database for that image.

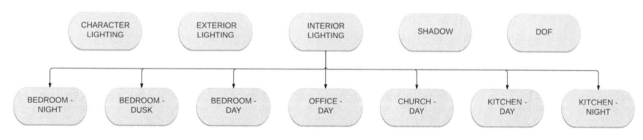

Figure 2.19 Flow chart of a sample directory structure of a reference library.

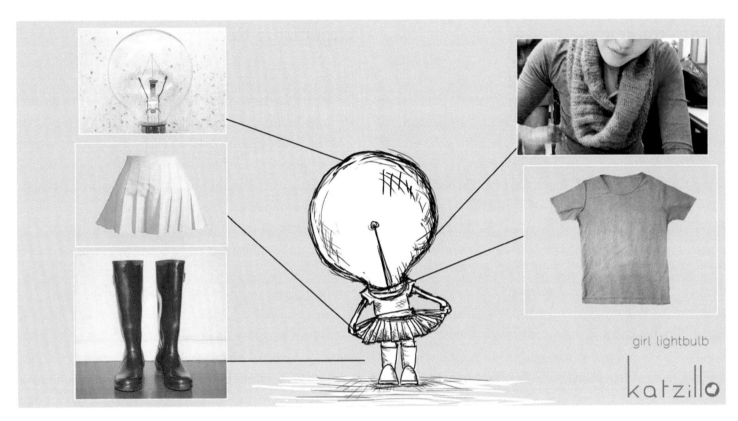

girl lightbulb

katzillo

Figure 2.20 An example of a character style sheet.

Another good use of reference is to create a style sheet which combines similar references on a minimal number of pages. These sheets can be easily referenced and followed by all the artists on the team. This is something an artist is highly encouraged to do when creating characters, props, or environments because it allows for ideas to be fleshed out and a better, more concrete understanding to be formed.

Final Thoughts

Reference images are just the starting point to a great image and the artist does not have to match to it perfectly. The artist is free to make aesthetic decisions and create visual styles all his or her own. But by gathering and analyzing reference, the artist is able to have a solid foundation to construct beautiful images.

Interview
with **Sharon Calahan**

Lighting Director of Photography :: Pixar Animation Studios.

Q. What is your current job/role at your company?
A. I work for Pixar Animation Studios as a Lighting Director of Photography.

Q. What inspired you to become an artist on CG films?
A. I knew at a very young age that I wanted to be an artist, even before I was old enough to go to kindergarten. In particular, I was drawn to animation because naturally that is the type of entertainment I was exposed to at the time, especially whatever was playing on *The Wide World of Disney* on TV. Many years later, I was working as an art director in broadcast television when CG animation was in its infancy. The first time I saw a flying logo, the potential seemed infinite, and I was hooked.

Q. What are your main sources of inspiration and reference? Do you prefer to go into the real world and observe or do you look to photography or more traditional artwork?
A. I try not to limit myself; inspiration can come from anywhere at any time. I try to be open to whatever I stumble across. It is a combination of seeing the world through the interpretation of other artists combined with observing the world myself. Movies and paintings particularly resonate with me, and I enjoy looking at great photography and stage productions.

Q. We have read that you have traveled to various locations for look development reference and inspiration for your films, specifically *Cars 2*. What is the benefit to seeing your reference in person as opposed to just finding photographs or other images online?

A. Online photo reference is great. We use it heavily to pre-scout a research trip to know where to go and what might be interesting, and it is often useful for when visiting a location isn't practical. But it isn't the same thing as seeing it yourself. When Harley and I went to Paris for *Ratatouille*, we of course did our online research first. While there, we both took a lot of photographs that we exchanged when we returned. It was astounding to see how we each viewed that environment from a different point of view. We found many unexpected surprises that we would have never found looking online or in books. How would I know that the fountain I'm looking at has rainbow-like highlights unless I am able to walk around it and observe the light changing? How would I know how variable the weather is in October without watching it change every five minutes? How would I notice the little touches of light quality: the softness, the modulation by the tree leaves, the piles of rusty brown leaves on the cobblestones, the warmth from reflected light between buildings? By experiencing the world through physically being there, I can shoot photos from my own point of view, composing, exposing and processing them to capture the qualities that I want to remember and evoke. And perhaps more importantly, I gain an emotional connection to the environment and memories that lets me know when an image feels "right." For *Ratatouille* we were trying to capture Paris, for *Cars 2* we needed to find the essential truths for several countries, finding ways to contrast them to make each unique.

Q. As a painter, do you approach lighting differently in your paintings from how you would a 3D scene? Or do you take a similar approach?

A. When I am painting, especially when I'm painting on location, the process is really an exercise in close observation and working quickly enough to capture the light before it changes. I'm not thinking very much; rather, I'm reacting to what I'm seeing. I'm not trying to create a finished painting. I'm studying the effects of light and how to best represent them, with varying degrees of success because I'm often struggling with the more technical aspects of painting with oil on canvas. If I am painting in the studio, I'm trying to go deeper into that observation and trying to improve upon what I painted in the field, but usually still trying to be quite literal with it. It is an introspective process. When I'm creating lighting for a film, the process is much more complex, collaborative, dynamic and externally focused. The lighting needs to convey emotion and visual information to the viewer in a way that best serves the story. It might be highly theatrical or stylized. Certainly, there is some overlap, and each inspires and informs the other. The basic principles of good image making are relevant for each. I feel that the most significant similarity is in the effort to create a solid value structure to reduce unnecessary information, thus highlighting what is important.

Q. What non-CG artwork inspires you?

A. I particularly enjoy viewing art that is very different from what I am able to create or from how I view the world. It challenges me to rethink my point of view and to keep learning.

Q. What do you think is lighting's largest contribution to an animated film?

A. When I am trying to explain what I do to somebody unfamiliar with CG, animation or even live-action filmmaking, I simplify my explanation to the bare essential: light creates order out of chaos. I show them an unlit image juxtaposed with a lit one and explain how we use light to direct the eye to the action; and how light, shadow, and color are used to create a mood.

Q. Where do you think the future of lighting is headed?

A. As computers have become faster, the tools have evolved to be capable of a much greater approximation of reality. It is easy to see this trend continuing and becoming more real time in interaction.

Q. If you could tell yourself one piece of advice when you were first starting out in this industry, what would it be?

A. As a first pass, I answered this question with a list, because I could write an entire book on this topic. But as I mulled it over, it became clear that there was one essential bit of advice that acts as an umbrella over all others: "Be curious."

Q. In your opinion, what makes a good lighting artist?

A. Passion. A person who loves to light and to make beautiful images is a joy to work with.

3

The Lighter's Toolbox

Lighting in CG is done by positioning virtual lights around an environment with either an interactive Graphic User Interface (GUI) or through code. Although there are many differences between these CG lights and real world lights, it is easiest to think about lighting for animation as one would stage lighting. Both start with a dark set filled with characters and props. It is then the lighting artist's job to add lights of varying quality to illuminate the stage. Both have the goal of illuminating the necessary parts of the scene while setting the mood for the audience.

CG lights and the renderers are generally constructed to mimic how light reacts in the real world. They can often simulate elements like rays of light bouncing off one surface onto another and light refracting through glass objects and liquids. The main difference is that CG lights have the ability to detach from the laws of physics, granting the artist complete control over their attributes. For example, CG lights generally have the option to turn shadow casting off. This would be impossible to do for a real light source and can give the artist more flexibility to do what is necessary to create aesthetically pleasing images.

Common CG Lights

Before lighting in a CG world, artists must know what virtual lights are available to them. These lights are tools at artists' disposal designed to give them everything necessary to craft a well-lit image. The lights listed in this section are not software specific but are commonly found in almost all renderers. They may go by different names but, regardless of whether it is the simplest software package on the market or the most robust proprietary renderer in a massive studio, the characteristics and uses remain the same. This section will not only work to describe how these lights function and their attributes but will also aim to show specific situations when each type of light is appropriate.

Point Lights

A point light is the simplest CG light to understand. Point lights are placed in a scene at a given X, Y, and Z coordinate and they radiate light in all directions. In other words, the artist places a point light in a given spot and light rays shoot out from that point in every direction. If shadows are enabled on the light they will also be cast radially from the position of the point light.

Point lights are best used when simulating something like a candle or a bare light bulb. They are lights that are small in size and illuminate in all directions and are especially useful when the light source is actually on screen. In this situation, the point light can be seen shooting light in all directions and the resulting shadows will replicate what would happen in the natural world.

Since point lights are so conceptually straightforward, new artists commonly overuse them. A new artist sees a part of the image in need of light and will place a point light in that area. The problem is that not only can a point light look incorrect, it can be inefficient and cause unnecessary render calculations. When a point light is positioned off camera, only a small segment of the rays being emitted are actually used. Therefore, the rays being cast away from the scene can still calculate light and shadow values which will slow down render times immensely.

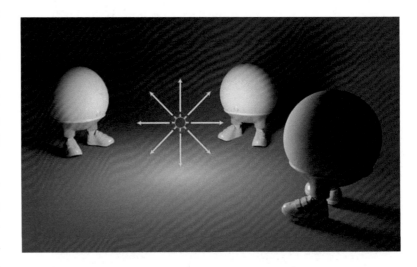

Figure 3.1 Point lights are placed in a scene at a given X, Y, and Z coordinate and they radiate light in all directions.

Directional Lights

Directional or distant lights cast light rays in one designated direction. They emanate light across the entire CG scene following the angle determined by the lighting artist. Therefore, the only positional attribute that matters in regard to a directional light is the rotation. The X, Y, Z position and the size of the directional light in the scene do not matter. By design, directional lights simulate any light that is very far away from the scene and illuminates across the entire shot. Because of this, some artists prefer to use directional lights when simulating sun or moonlight. Directional lights can be quite useful as gentle fill lights as well.

The major holdup for using a directional light is the fact that it illuminates everything uniformly. As discussed previously, any time uniform lighting exists in a scene the image runs the risk of losing visual shaping and overall interest. It is often important when using directional lights to implement gobos (discussed later) or other methods to vary the intensity of the light to avoid this issue.

Directional lights also have issues with regards to shadows. They can have very limited control over the softness and look of the shadows when compared with spotlights. Also, they can be inefficient since many of the light rays being cast will never be seen on camera and therefore could add to render calculations with no visual improvements.

Spotlights

Spotlights are very common in many renderers. They are similar to a point light in that they have no physical dimensions but are different because they illuminate in a specific direction inside a conical area. Spotlights are popular because an artist can use a

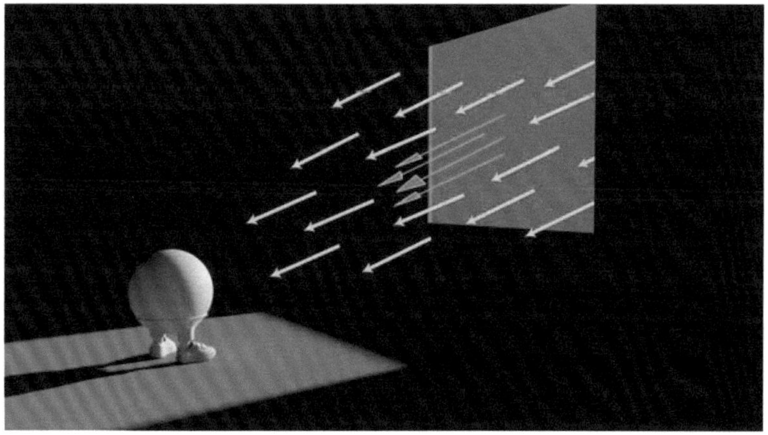

Figure 3.2 Directional or distant lights cast light rays in one designated direction.

Figure 3.3 Spotlights are similar to a point light in that they have no physical dimensions but are different because they illuminate in a specific direction inside a conical area.

spotlight to specifically sculpt light into an area of the scene. The cone can be centered on one specific object leaving the audience focusing on what the lighter wants. They also have the benefit of additional controls not found in other lights, like the ability to project a mapped image onto the scene and the ability to make their beam of light visible as if passing through dust or fog. Spotlights also wield the most control over the shadow settings and allow the artist the ability to simulate almost any shadow type. Unlike point lights or directional lights, spotlights produce fewer light rays that are wasted by being fired off screen. Ultimately, spotlights give the artist the most control over the look of the light and will increase the render efficiency of the scene and minimize render times.

Spotlights have a wide array of uses. They can be used as flashlights, streetlights, stage spotlights, or in other scenarios where light starts off at one point and emits in a conical shape. In practice their range reaches far beyond that. A spotlight can often be placed far away from the scene to simulate the sun or moon. Their cone can be focused on the scene and be much more efficient than a directional light. Spotlights can be used to represent an off camera lamp or fireplace since the artist can focus their influence back into the scene. They are also often used to simulate indirect light and color spill because of their ability to isolate light to specific regions.

Ultimately, the spotlight is one of the most versatile weapons in the lighting artist's arsenal. It can be controlled and manipulated to simulate almost all lighting situations. If using it well, the artist can utilize the benefits of the spotlight to craft a fine looking image.

Area Lights

An area light is a light source that emits light from a geometric shape and is, in many cases, the best representation of a real world light source. The shape is generally a 2D plane, but some software packages allow for light to be emitted from a variety of shapes. Some software packages automatically calculate area lights with decay, which is very different from other lights discussed thus far. This decay causes lights to decrease in intensity as they travel over a distance. It is also common for the amount of light emitted from an area light to increase as the size of the light grows.

Area lights are soft by nature since they are usually larger light sources than point lights or spotlights. They cast soft shadows and large specular highlights to create this soft overall look. Area lights are often used to replicate monitors, television screens, or large, flat fluorescent lights. Another common use for area lights is to be used to generate highlight specs or reflections in eyes or reflective surfaces.

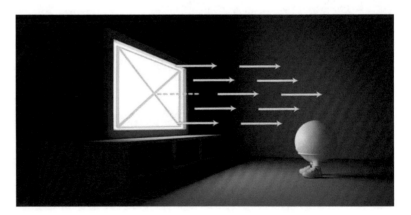

Figure 3.4 Area lights emit light from a geometric shape onto their surroundings.

When creating an area light, it is important to ensure that it is only casting light in the one direction needed. Some software packages default to area lights emitting in both directions, but limiting it to only one side often cuts render calculations in half.

One main downside to area lights' soft shadows is that they are difficult to process and can be taxing on the renderer. Because of this, the addition of an area light can increase a scene's render time dramatically. As hardware and renderers become more powerful this is becoming less of an issue and area lights' usage is on the rise.

Ambient Lights

Ambient lights do not exist in the natural world. By default, ambient lights illuminate all objects in the scene evenly and do not cast shadow or show any directionality. The closest real world example of an ambient light is on an overcast day where the clouds completely block the sun and everything is more uniformly lit throughout the environment. Even in this situation, there is still more directionality and shadow casting than exists in a true CG ambient light. Artists have often advised against using ambient lights as they will result in the scene looking flat and unrealistic. If applied subtly and with a soft touch, ambient lights can be used to lift the darkest of values in a scene and help the final image.

Some software packages offer increased controls for an ambient light that allow the artist to give some shaping qualities. The artist can create ambient shade which will give the light directionality based on its position in the scene and the ability to cast ambient shadows. With these controls in place, ambient light can be used to simulate large areas of bounce light or overhead illumination from the sky.

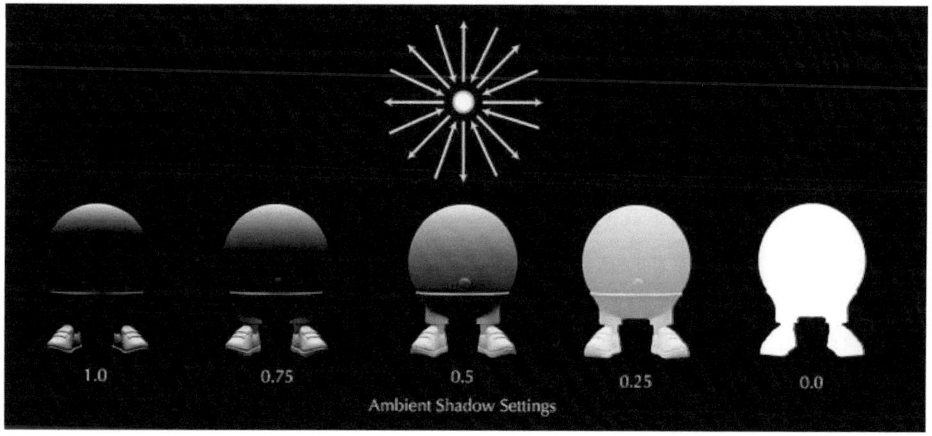

Figure 3.5 Ambient lights do not exist in the natural world. By default, ambient lights illuminate all objects in the scene evenly and do not cast shadow or show any directionality.

Basic Properties of Light

All the lights in the scene need to be meticulously crafted to fit their role within the shot. To obtain this level of sophisticated adjustments the software package gives the artist a series of controls to modify the properties of a particular light source and its shadow. This section aims to define many of the light properties and give a sense of how each one can be used.

Color

All light in the real world has color. Whether it is natural or man-made, light will always cast some shade of warm or cool light. The sun projects warm light, fluorescent light has a green tint, and a television emits an animated array of light colors. Even though light in the real world almost always has color, the default color of light in almost all renderers is white. Therefore it is absolutely essential for CG lights to adjust the light color in order to create a successful final image.

The color of a CG light can be represented in different ways. The first and most prominent is RGB values. RGB values refer to the additive method of color which uses a mixture of red (R), green (G), and blue (B) to create any color in the spectrum. If all three colors

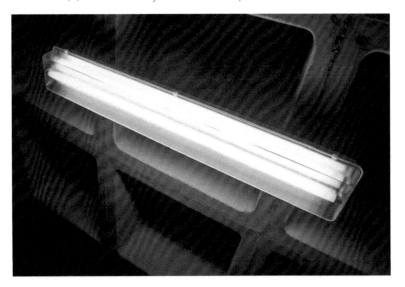

Figure 3.6 Depending on the light source, light color can change dramatically from the orange glow of a sunny day to the green cast of a fluorescent light.

are turned up to full capacity, the resulting color is white. If all three are set to 0, the result is black. If all values were the same, then the color would be a range of gray values. When the numbers differ, that is when visual color values begin to emerge.

These numbers can be represented on a scale of either 0 to 1 or 0 to 255. The 0 to 1 scale is simply the percentage of that color's contribution. If the color desired is red, the number would be 1 0 0 since the contribution of red would be 100 percent and green and blue would be 0 percent. The 0 to 255 scale works the same way except the numbers are not percentages but whole values that represent the entire range of colors in an eight-bit image.

Additionally, colors can be represented in the HSV (hue, saturation, value) or HSL (hue, saturation, lightness) method. These methods describe color as it appears on the color spectrum by identifying the color's hue, how robust it is, and how bright it is. The hue is a numeric value from 0 to 1 (or sometimes 0 to 360) that defines where a hue exists on the color wheel. Numbers 0 and 1 are normally red and all numbers in between represent a different hue. The saturation indicates how dull or pure the color is and the value is how light or how dark.

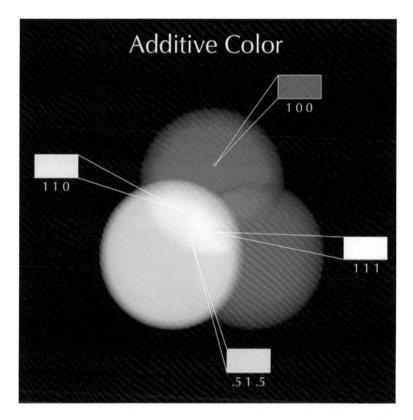

Figure 3.7 An additive color chart with examples of colors and their values.

Figure 3.8 A chart showing the how changing the hue, saturation, or value can affect the color.

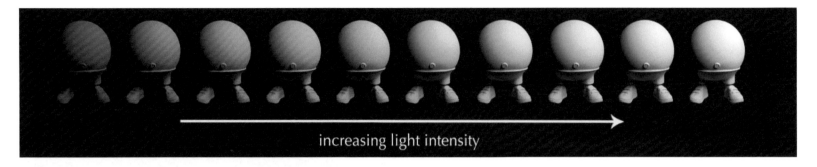

increasing light intensity

Figure 3.9 Light intensity is a multiplier of the color and is one of the most influential light settings.

diffuse

specular

Figure 3.10 Isolating diffuse and specular illumination and showing how they work together in the final image.

Intensity

Dialing in the intensity so the values are just right is a huge part of the lighter's responsibilities. It is not only about illuminating areas of the scene, but crafting areas of light and darkness to direct the viewer's eye and create visual interest throughout the shot.

Technically speaking, intensity is simply a multiplier of color. When a light has an intensity of 1 and a color of white (1 1 1), that means the color being emanated from the light is pure white. When intensity is set to 0.5, the RGB values of the light color are cut in half (0.5 0.5 0.5). When the intensity is 2, they are doubled (2 2 2).

Diffuse Illumination vs. Specular Illumination

CG lights influence two different types of illumination on the surface material of objects: specular illumination and diffuse illumination. Diffuse illumination is the matte lighting across the surface of the object. The diffuse illumination generally makes up a larger, broader area of light on the object. Specular illumination is the highlights, or the small, bright, shiny area, of an object with a reflective surface. Together, they combine to create the overall lighting on an object.

Most software packages allow the artist the ability to control the specular and diffuse contributions individually in order to craft the look. As will be seen in future chapters, there may be times when the artist creates a light to emit only specular or diffuse values to achieve the look he or she is striving for.

Light Decay

As mentioned in Chapter 2, all real world light sources only illuminate for a certain distance. They naturally decay and lose intensity as they travel and eventually reduce down to nothing. CG lights, in most renderers, do not function this way. In many render software packages they illuminate indefinitely. Software packages offer controls to allow the artist to let a light decay in a way that is much more natural. These controls may be called drop-off, falloff, decay, or light decay depending on the rendering software. For the purposes of this book, this phenomenon will be referred to as decay. CG lights turn decay off by default because it greatly increases the render times and, in most situations, the audience will never perceive that decay in space.

The rate of decay can vary to allow for different types of mathematical calculations. As the decay rate is increased, the light rays will reduce and eliminate more quickly. Therefore, a linear decay rate will

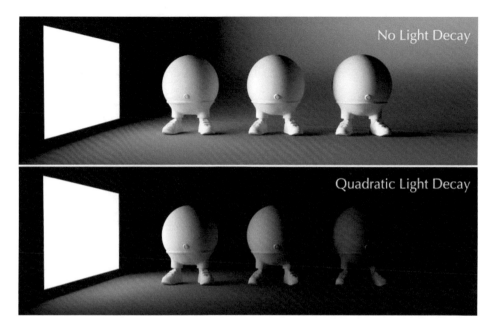

Figure 3.11 By enabling decay the artist can make a light appear more realistic as its value will decrease as objects get further away from it.

last longer than a greater decay rate like cubic or quadratic. Take note that as decay is added to the light, the light's intensity may have to increase dramatically in order to compensate.

Figure 3.12 Volumetric lights can make it appear as if the light is passing through dust, mist, or other material that makes the light rays visible.

Volumetric Light

Software packages will also give the artist the ability to make light visible to the viewer. In nature this can happen if light is passing through dust or fog and the rays can become visible. In CG, this phenomenon can be called visible lights, volume lights, or, in some instances, God rays or crepuscular rays. For the purpose of this book, it will be called volumetric light. Volumetric light is most generally applied to spotlights as they can best harness and implement the volumetric light most effectively. When used properly, light fog can add drama or a "wow" factor to a shot.

Shadows

Shadows are simply areas of blocked light. Shadows can be poetically described as dark, ominous shapes that follow people around but they are not objects unto themselves. So they are more the absence of light versus the addition of darkness. The aesthetic roles of shadows will be discussed in later chapters, but this section will discuss the technical ins and outs of shadows.

Types of Shadows

There are two main types of shadows that exist in computer graphics: cast shadow and ambient shadow. Cast shadows are the elongated shadows that mimic the shape of the object. Their source normally can be pinpointed to one light and they fall in the direction opposite the light.

I am a cast shadow

I am an ambient shadow

Figure 3.13 Demonstrating the difference between ambient shadows and cast shadows.

What is Shadows' Visual Contribution?

Shadows contribute greatly to the overall final look of a shot. Primarily, shadows help define spatial relationships. Without shadows, it can often be difficult to determine whether one object is in front of or behind another. Also, it makes it is impossible to determine if an object is touching another surface or floating above.

A well-crafted shadow can also supply a much-needed dark section to a shot. Oftentimes lighting artists need to create a dark section behind a character in order to get that character to visually pop off the screen and that can be done with a well-placed shadow. In other words, shadows and their placement can be constructed within the scene to allow for the best visual storytelling.

Shadows are also beneficial in helping the audience understand the environment the characters exist in and the time of day. This is not something that the audience is necessarily aware of but instead it is certainly something that is sensed. A long shadow with parallel lines will clue the audience that the shot is taking place outside, either late in the day or in the early morning when the sun is closer to the ground. A very large shadow behind a character will indicate the light source is much closer to the subject and therefore being lit by something other than the sun or moon.

Figure 3.14 Shadows can help define spatial relationships between objects.

short shadow

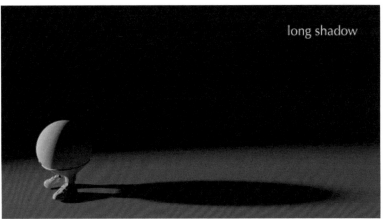
long shadow

Figure 3.15 The length of the cast shadow can also help the audience identify the time of day or the overall lighting scenario.

Shadow Qualities

Shadow Size

Shadow size is based on a few determining factors. First is the angle of the light. The lower the light is relative to the object, the longer the shadow. The more overhead or perpendicular the light is relative to the subject, the shorter the shadow. In other words, the subject's shadow will be much longer at sunrise or sunset than it is at high noon.

The distance between the light and the subject influences the resulting size of the shadow. Generally speaking, the further the light source is away from the subject, the smaller the shadow will appear. A light source that is very close to an object, like a candle or a flashlight, will create a very large shadow. A very distant light source, like the sun, will create a relatively much smaller shadow.

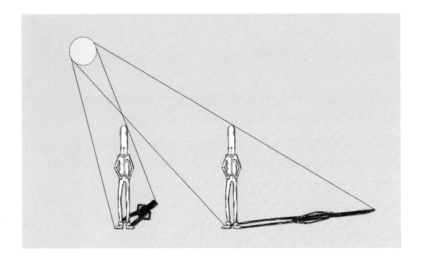

Figure 3.16 As the sun is high in the sky during the afternoon hours, the shadow length is relatively short. During morning or evening, as the sun is closer to the horizon, the shadow length will be much longer.

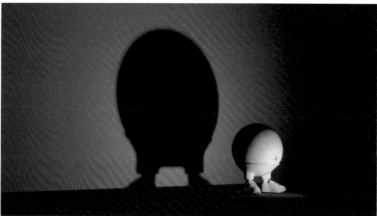

Figure 3.17 The closer an object is to a light source the larger that object's shadow will appear to be. As the object moves further from that light source, the shadow will shrink in size.

Shadow Color

Shadows are often thought of as being black but that is rarely the case. They will almost always have at least some color value in them. Remember, in the real world shadows are nothing but an object blocking one or more light sources. That means the remaining light sources that are not completely blocked will hit the shadowed region and contribute to the color of that shadowed area.

Take a sunny day, for example (Figure 3.18). The sun would come down and hit the subject, casting a shadow onto the ground. The shadow would be the absence of the sunlight's value and therefore contain none of that warm light contribution. The shadow would, however, still be lit from all of the blue sky surrounding the scene. Therefore, shadows on bright sunny days definitely have a distinct blue cast.

Figure 3.18 In this sunny day example, the shadow has a cooler cast that is being determined by the sky color.

Shadow Softness

Similar to shadow size, shadow softness is determined by the relative size of the light source in comparison to the object. The larger the relative size of the light source, the softer the light. This is true because the larger the light source, the greater the number of angles at which the light rays can reach the subject. This widely varying incoming light gets scattered over a greater area and therefore is perceived to be softer. If the light source is very small and far away, the shadow will not have this softness and be much harder around the edges. Think of shadow puppets. If the hands are closer to the light source the shadow is softer than when the hands are further away.

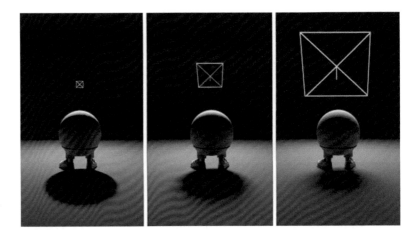

Figure 3.19 The larger the light source is relative to the object, the softer the shadow that is cast.

Light Properties for Shadows
Gobos

Shadow casting can be expensive to render. There are a couple of methods lighters use to simulate additional shadows in the scene without increasing render times. Creating a gobo or cookie cutter for a light is one of these methods. Gobos or cookies are based on the photographic principle of placing an object in front of the light source to cast a shadow onto the scene. The term "gobo" is derived from either the phrase "Go Between" or the acronym for "Goes Before Optics." In most software packages, gobos can be accomplished by mapping an image file onto the color channel of the particular light. The image map will be projected through the light and the resulting dark shapes will appear in frame, creating the simulated shadow. Both still frames and an animated sequence of frames could be used.

Figure 3.20 Gobos or cookies are based on the photographic principle of placing an object in front of the light source to cast a shadow onto the scene.

Gobos are also a quick way of implying what is happening off screen without actually building geometry. The artist can project the shadow of a building, some trees, or even other characters through gobos. In that way gobos allow an artist to expand the CG world without costly additional geometry.

It must be remembered that gobos are 2D solutions to a 3D issue. They can look flat, unrealistic, and pasted onto a scene if not painted correctly. It is best to not rely on gobos too heavily, but when added with restraint and crafted with care they can be a powerful tool.

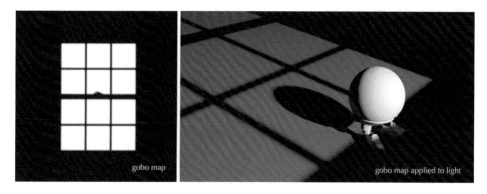

gobo map

gobo map applied to light

Figure 3.21 Gobo maps can be painted textures that are applied to a light's color and projected onto the scene.

Final Thoughts

These are the main tools that every lighter has at his or her disposal. Professional lighters at animation studios do not have a secret vault filled with different lights or settings or "make it pretty" buttons. They work with spotlights, gobos, and raytraced renderers just like a student. The key is to learn how to utilize all of the attributes of these lights in such a way as to make successful final images.

Interview
with Andrew Beddini

Technical Supervisor of Imaging :: Blue Sky Studios.

Q. What is your current job/role at your company?

A. I'm the Technical Supervisor of Imaging at Blue Sky Studios. I work with the back end TD departments to ensure that our imagery meets a visual standard of excellence while simultaneously assessing cost and value to ensure we don't spend extra on something our audience won't see.

Q. What inspired you to become an artist on CG films?

A. During my last semester of my industrial design degree, I found myself slightly disillusioned with my job prospects. I really enjoyed design, but my portfolio at the time demonstrated a significant aptitude for an industry demand for photorealistic product renderings. The only job offers I was receiving were for positions where I'd be shackled to a computer to simply draft and make pretty pictures of someone else's designs. Certainly not the end of the world, but I knew I would have very limited opportunities to express my creativity. A concerned professor of mine suggested that I get in touch with a former colleague of his who was then a CG supervisor at ILM. Within a few minutes of him looking at my portfolio, this gentlemen had me convinced my talents would be going to waste in the ID design world, and would be put to much better use in the VFX world. After that significant moment of inspiration, I created a self-taught graduate curriculum, chained myself to the university supercomputer for almost two years, and then landed my first job in the industry.

Q. What non-CG artwork inspires you?

A. I still gravitate towards design and architecture for inspiration. Architectural drawings by Hugh Ferriss and shape studies by Lebbeus Woods still blow me away. A friend of mine introduced me to Walton Ford recently, and I found his Audubon-style paintings with all of their subtle irony and humor to be pretty inspiring.

Q. What do you think is lighting's largest contribution to an animated film?

A. Hands down, setting the "mood." While an audience member will consciously connect with the animation performance and dialogue of a film, it's lighting's job to subconsciously influence that same audience member to register the mood of the scene via lighting techniques.

Q. Where do you think the future of lighting is headed?

A. On a shot level, full real time global illumination. We are getting pretty close to that, and we will owe the success of it to the new breed of renderers that will be able to take advantage of the bleeding edge 100+ core CPUs and co-processors just entering the market place. From a more overarching pipeline perspective, simultaneous real time multi-shot lighting for animated features. With the expected gains in per shot rendering, I see a day soon where one artist can light an entire sequence of shots simultaneously, relying heavily on intelligent automated management of the individual shot assets and scripts. Sort of a shot management "auto-pilot" where it allows the lighter more time to be an artist, and not a technician.

Q. Can you tell us why it is so important to be mindful of render times?

A. Well, it depends on the project, but in a feature-length animated film, establishing an acceptable range for render times is critical to the financial success of a film. Lighting decisions have a directly correlated impact on the shared machine resources throughout the whole studio. If a lighter fails to create an efficient lighting setup, not only will it affect their iterative and final rendering times for the affected shots, but it also takes away rendering resources from other artists that need them. That imbalance can lead to unanticipated purchases of more hardware, longer schedules, and a need for temp artists, which all could make or break a film.

Q. What are some techniques you would recommend to someone optimizing their lighting/render workflow?
A. Well,

- Don't try to perfect everything within the render; if your output is mono then you can solve a huge number of issues by easily addressing the problem in post/comp.
- Don't try to make everything perfect. Perfection is unattainable, so focus on what your audience will be looking at.
- Focus your time and attention on the eyes of a character. The audience connects to the character via the eyes, so don't let your workflow skimp on them.
- If you're working on multiple shots, learn how to script. Manipulating files via an automated/semi-automated script will save you time.

Q. If you could tell yourself one piece of advice when you were first starting out in this industry, what would it be?
A. Use your youth and lack of dependants to be as mobile as possible in the infancy of your career. Working at multiple studios will not only expose you to a plethora of techniques and workflows, it will also increase your salary much faster than it would if you stayed in one place.

Q. In your opinion, what makes a good lighting artist?
A. From my eighteen years in the industry, I can say the most successful lighting artists have had a limitless ability to visually and technically problem-solve without guidance from a superior. The old adage "he/she just gets it" really rings true. Lighting supervisors and leads are thrilled when you can complete shots with minimal intervention from them. If you can't figure out what's wrong with a shot from either a visual or technical perspective without hand holding, you're gonna have problems.

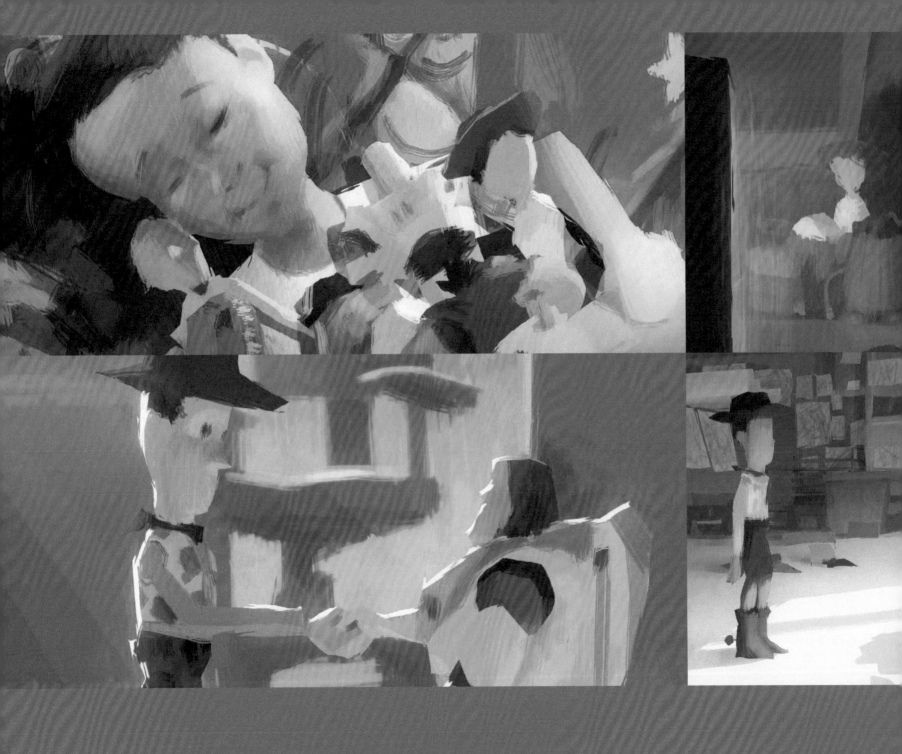

4

The Lighter's Workflow

The previous chapter focused on what tools the artist has available in software packages. This chapter will focus on how to use them. It will stress the importance of establishing a lighting workflow that enables the artist to be as efficient and effective as possible. This workflow will be explained from pre-lighting to work-in-progress lighting and through final render. The more efficient the workflow, the more lighting iterations the artist will be able to output before the deadline which ultimately leads to the best-looking images.

This chapter will cover various workflow methods. © Disney.

Pre-lighting

Before beginning any project, the first thing the artist should do is create or gather reference. The specifics of how to gather, organize, and process reference were discussed in Chapter 2, but the importance of this step cannot be reiterated enough. Always use reference!

Creating Color Keys and Mockups

After reference images have been gathered, it is important for the artist to create mockups and/or color keys as a blueprint for the lighting he or she hopes to achieve. At larger studios an art department or design artists could provide this, but in many cases the lighter will design and create these on his or her own.

Color keys show the overall color palette for a sequence of shots or a project in terms of the key direction and overall lighting quality through a handful of example images. They can be done digitally as well as in fine art mediums such as watercolors, colored charcoal, colored pencils, and even in crayons. Color keys are standard at larger animation houses but all projects, regardless of scope, can benefit from these visual designs. They certainly don't have to be highly detailed or specific because they are meant to give an overall impression. Art directors have even suggested keeping the color keys thumbnail sized since, if their structure will work at that scale, they will work at a larger size. Color keys are important assets that will ultimately give the artist a strong understanding of the visual script of the project.

Once a color key is established, the next stage is to mockup and design the lighting for the shot. The fastest and most accessible mockup is the quick sketch. A quick sketch is a good way to get thoughts onto paper to begin fleshing out ideas. These sketches could be simple diagrams from a bird's eye view laying out the positions of the lights or even crude stick people. The purpose is to start expressing the idea visually to better communicate the possibilities for the overall look.

Figure 4.1 Color Key and Concept Art from the animated short *The Fantastic Flying Books of Mr. Morris Lessmore*. Property of Moonbot Studios.

Preparing the Shot

The set is built, the character is animated, and through the use of reference and color keys the artist has a good idea of how the image will look. The shot is ready to go! So what is next? Whether one is a new lighter or a seasoned pro, this moment can be daunting.

The first step is to modify the render settings to allow the shot to function as efficiently as possible during the early testing process. When first setting up the shot, render settings should be lowered. Anti-aliasing can be scaled back, render samples can be reduced, and motion blur turned off. The main goal of these modifications is to ensure the iterated, work-in-progress (WIP) renders will run as quickly as possible. In these beginning stages of lighting, the artist wants to make many adjustments to establish the general look of the shot without being hindered by waiting for long renders to see the results. Having slow work-in-progress renders is deflating to the artist because it leads to lack of focus and a slow turnaround.

The artist also needs to determine the image aspect ratio. The aspect ratio is the relative size of the height and width of the image. Video resolution is a 4:3 (640 x 480) aspect ratio, but that is being used less frequently. HD aspect ratios have become increasingly more common among monitors and other displays. These aspect ratios are closer to 16:9

and are normally 1280 x 720 or 1920 x 1080. In film, these aspect ratios can stretch even wider to allow for a more cinematic and dramatic look. In *Ben Hur* (1959), the screen was stretched to a ratio of 2.75:1.

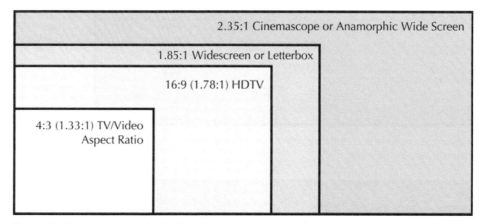

Figure 4.2a Common aspect ratios for film and television.

Figure 4.2b Wide aspect ratios like this one can provide a more cinematic and dramatic look to a film. © mptvimages.com.

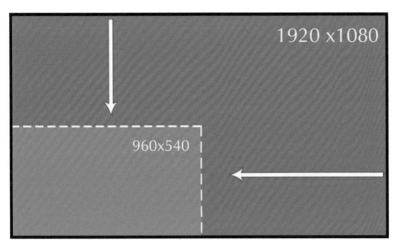

Figure 4.3 By reducing the size of the image the artist can greatly reduce render times and optimize his or her workflow.

Figure 4.4 Isolating the render to only the area the artist is focused on is also an effective optimization tool.

Once the resolution and aspect ratio is determined, the artist should decrease the size of the overall render to reduce the render time when doing test renders. Generally, WIP frames do not need to be larger than 600 pixels in any dimension in order for the artist to make accurate observations about most of the lighting. This is often a decrease in size of the final render setting by 50–75 percent, but that is completely normal. Scaling the image down to 50 percent of the height and 50 percent of the width can reduce render times down to a quarter of the original. This step can save the artist huge amounts of time, allowing him or her to focus on the lighting and spend less time waiting for renders.

Most renderers also give the artist the option of rendering only sections of the frame. If the artist is only working on the lights for a character on the far left side of the screen, rendering the entire frame is unproductive. By isolating the area that is required, turnaround time on the frames increases rapidly due to eliminating unnecessary processing and analysis.

At this point, the artist would also be wise to turn off any geometry that is not influencing the look of the scene. If the scene is taking place in the forest, make sure the forest is pruned down to exclude extra, unnecessary set pieces. Only the objects that are visible to the camera or are close enough to cast shadow into the scene should be included. All other set pieces can be removed. This can be done for cities and even interiors as rooms are not visible in the scene and can have their geometry removed to make the scene more efficient.

Linear vs. sRGB

Fully understanding linear workflow is an incredibly dense topic that could populate an entire book on its own. From the artist's perspective, working with the linear workflow produces a greater range of values in the image. The dark values will contain more variation and a softer transition to true black. The lighter parts of the image will also have a greater range of white values as well, which will give the artist more control when compositing the image and doing final color adjustments.

To understand the linear workflow one must understand gamma. Gamma is an adjustment to any image that only influences the midpoints and leaves the white point set to 1 and black to 0. Gamma controls start off by 1 at default. If that value is raised the midpoints darken, and if it is lowered the midpoints brighten. By default most monitors or displays users interact with are adjusted and given a gamma setting of 2.2.

In other words, all the images seen on almost every computer monitor are adjusted darker than they should be. So why do humans not perceive this? It is because every digitized image is counterbalanced against this adjustment and therefore appears relatively correct on screen. By working in linear workspace, the artist is choosing to break this double correction and work without it.

It is during this pre-lighting phase that the artist should determine whether to work with a linear workflow or sRGB. This may depend on the software package being used or the final destination for the images being created. Either way, since the rendered image will look distinctly different using these two methods, the artist should make this decision prior to lighting. Switching to a linear

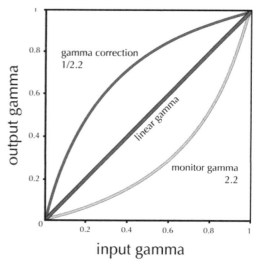

Figure 4.5 Normally, an image is gamma corrected to match the monitor's shifting color. By working in a linear workflow the artist is able to bypass that process and generate a greater range of values.

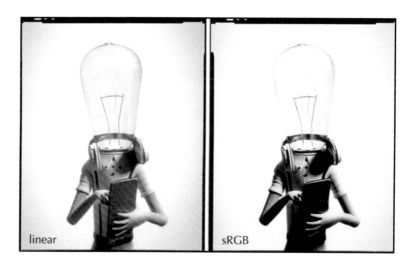

Figure 4.6 The image on the left is using the linear workflow while the image on the right is not.

workflow while a shot is being lit will require the artist to go back and make adjustments to all colored texture maps, which is incredibly time consuming and tedious.

Many major animation studios work with some form of a linear workflow and can have it embedded into the pipeline. Although some software packages work in linear workflow out of the box, most individual users and small studios will be required to set up that workflow themselves. Every software package has a different way of creating this workflow and often requires making adjustments to both the lights and the materials.

Understanding the Roles of Each Light

In the beginning it is essential to understand the tools that are available to the lighter. Next is understanding how each of these lights will be utilized. How will each light be placed around the scene in order for the artist to achieve the aesthetic goals? There is a standard way of lighting that was born out of photography and film that serves as the basis for CG terminology of lighting and its practices.

Key

Anyone familiar with film, theater, or photographic lighting will know the term "key light." The key light is the main or primary light source in the scene. It generally dominates the overall look and is responsible for the largest portion of illumination as well the dominant shadow in most circumstances. If it is an outdoor, daytime scene, then it is generally going to be the sun. For an interior scene,

it will be whatever artificial lamp or window is generating the majority of the overall lighting. The overall quality of the key light is the biggest contributor to the look of a shot. If the position of the key light is flattening the subject then it will be almost impossible to generate good shaping. Key lights are generally positioned to the side of the main subject relative to the camera in order to create variation. The lighter is obviously obligated to position the light where the story dictates but the goal is to never have the key too frontal because this will make the subject flat, except for the extremely rare case where that is desired. The color of the key is also incredibly important. If the color of the key light is off and makes the scene appear unappealing there is very little the other lights can do to counteract that. In other words, establishing a good key light with proper settings is the most important thing a lighter will do with each shot.

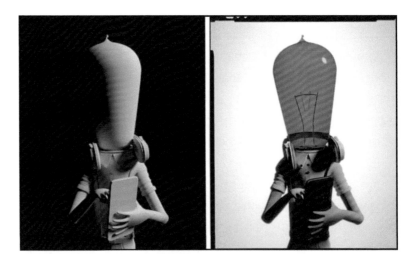

Figure 4.7 The image on the left is the character with all white materials and only the key light. The right image is the key as it appears in the final image.

Fill

The fill light is the key's complement and serves to add light value to shadow cast from the key. If the key light is coming in from one side, then the fill will complement that by "filling" in the dark parts on the screen-right side. This will enable the key's shadow to be lifted above pure black and allow it to achieve a look of believability.

The intensity and color of the fill light is completely dependent on the scene. Less intense fill lights are necessary for scenes with higher contrast levels while more intense fill lights can decrease contrast. That is why the overall contrast level of a shot can be termed as the "key to fill ratio."

The color of the fill light is dependent on the color of the environment surrounding the subject. Take, for example, the bright sunny day with a blue sky surrounding the subject. The fill light in this instance will be that same sky blue color and the shadows will be filled accordingly.

Bounce

Generally speaking, the key light comes from above the subject in most lighting scenarios. In outdoor scenes being lit by the sun or moon this is always the case. This is because the sun and moon are always above the horizon line. Characters, unless being depicted as evil, are not generally lit from underneath since this the look is unnatural and unflattering.

In natural lighting scenarios light from above the subject hits the ground below and causes secondary light rays to bounce up, filling in the dark areas on the underside of the subject. This type of secondary light is simulated with a light called the bounce light.

Figure 4.8 The image on the left is the character with all white materials and just the fill light. The right image is the key and the fill light as they appear in the final image.

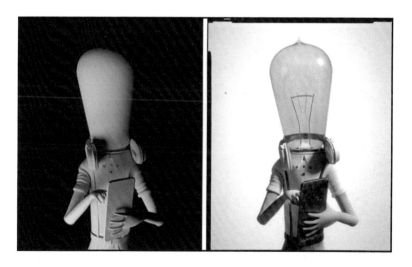

Figure 4.9 The image on the left is the character with all white materials and only the bounce light. The right image is the key light, the fill light, and the bounce light as they appear in the final image.

Bounce light is the broad, soft light that comes up from below. The intensity and color of the bounce is dependent on the intensity of the key and the surface it is bouncing off. The stronger the key and the more reflective the surface, the more pronounced the bounce light will be and the greater the color of the ground surface will influence the color of the bounce.

Rim/Kick

Here is where an artist can get into lights that exist merely for aesthetic reasons. The rim light exists to help separate the subject from the background and make its outline readable and prominent. Often the rim light is not driven by anything practical in the scene, but just a desire to make the subject's outline more readable.

This is particularly true when a character is holding a small object like a pencil or pointing his or her finger. A rim light can be implemented to better read the outline of that object and ensure the audience can see what is happening. Usually the rim light exists on the side opposite the key, but in a given situation it can also be successfully used on the key side as well.

Kick lights also fall into the category of lights normally based on strictly aesthetic goals and are similar to rim lights. They are lights positioned at low angles to help add additional variation to flatly lit areas. Kick lights are often utilized on the fill side of an object when the fill light becomes too diffuse or too flat in one region. They have been known to exist on the key side as well to provide a bit of additional shaping. Often the kick light will add just a bit of value, especially in regard to specular values, to the fill side of the subject.

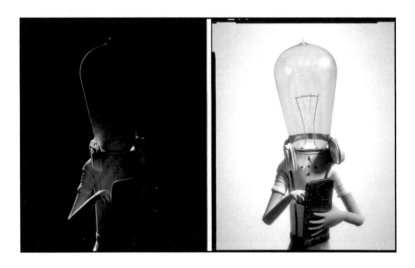

Figure 4.10 The image on the left is the character with all white materials and only the bounce light. The right image is the key light, the fill light, the bounce light, the kick light, and the rim light as they appear in the final image.

Utility

A utility light is any additional, practical light that exists in a scene that needs to be accounted for. These can be anything from glowing cell phone screens, flashlights, or police sirens. They are simply any other light in the scene used to show integration between all the light emitting sources and objects in the scene.

Figure 4.11 Four different shots that all benefit from utility lights. Still from the animated short *The Tale of Mr. Revus* (top left and bottom right), property of Marius Herzog. Still from the animated short *Edmond était un âne* (Edmond was a Donkey) (top right). Property of Papy3d/ONF NFB/ARTE. Still from the animated short *Little Freak* (bottom left). Property of Edwin Schaap.

Let There Be Light!

The prep work has been completed and now it is time to light. Beginning artists get overly excited by this process and start quickly adding all the lights they think they will need to the scene. They have a rough vision of how the scene is supposed to look and expect the first render to match this vision. Lighting does not work that way. Lighting takes time and patience. There may be a vision in the artist's mind, but it takes meticulous placement and adjustments to the settings for each light to reach that goal. To accomplish this, artists must establish a routine of slowly adding lights to the scene to systematically control the look of each and every one.

Creating Lights

Now that there is a firm understanding of the functions of the lights, it is time to start creating the light rig. The first step is to create the key light. There are many ways to accomplish this, but the following steps are a common method of positioning the key light.

1. Decide which light type works best to simulate the key light in the reference. Spotlight? Area light? Create the key light.
2. Put the key light in roughly the desired location within the scene.
3. Set the intensity and color to match the color key. (Do not feel pressured to get these attributes perfect. They will almost definitely need to be updated and modified once additional lights are added.)
4. Check the shadow being cast by the light to ensure it matches the reference's shape and softness.
5. Double check to ensure the previous adjustments did not hinder the shaping. There should be variations in values as the light moves across objects to show volume and space.
6. Verify that there are no extreme highlights or bright patches caused by the key light. The key should not be causing any area of the subject to be overly bright or blown out. This is because once all the other lights are added (fills, bounces, kicks, rims, and so on) their values will be added on top of the key's contribution and create a large, flat section of bright whites.

Once the key light is in place, move onto the next light in the scene and repeat until all of the basic lights have been created. A good order is to begin with the key then complement that light with a fill. Move on to the bounce light coming up from beneath and the sky light from above. Then finish up with any rims or kicks to help add definition and volume to the object. Also, construct any necessary utility lights at this point as they will greatly influence the attribute settings of the other lights and the overall final look.

Each light gets positioned with the same care as the key. Is the light creating any overly flat areas? Does the light match the intended look? Does the light's intensity cause any areas to go too bright and blow out? Does the color of the light accurately represent the surroundings? Some artists even prefer to make the light an exaggerated value like a bright red while positioning to help get a better understanding of that light's contribution. By adding lights one at a time, the artist should always be able to maintain control of each light's influence on the scene.

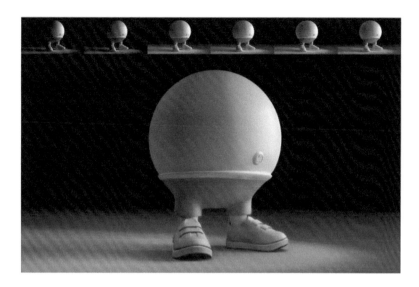

Figure 4.12 Example of adding each light to the scene individually and leaving them on as the artist adds the next one.

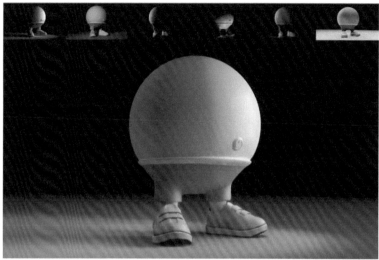

Figure 4.13 Example of adding each light to the scene individually and then turning it off before adding the next one.

Another method of working is to turn off all lights except the one being created so the artist knows exactly where it's being placed. For example, the artist would create the key as in the previous workflow. Then, when it is time to create the fill light, instead of leaving the key light on, the key light is turned off and the artist can just focus on the positioning of the fill light. The artist would repeat this process for each light until the end when all the lights are turned back on.

Once all the lights are roughly in place, it is time to analyze the overall look. Adjustments will be made to get all the lights to work together well. When making these adjustments, it is wise to change them one at a time to better understand how each modification is impacting the entire shot.

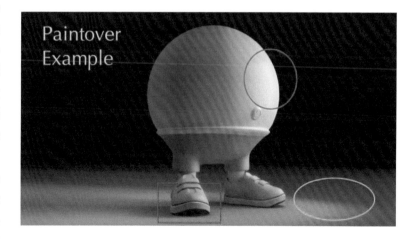

Figure 4.14 Once the image is complete the artist can analyze the results, critique the work, and begin to identify areas that can be improved upon.

Interactive Light Placement

Developing an efficient system for positioning lights is incredibly important to the process. One effective method commonly used is interactive light placement. This involves moving and positioning from the vantage point of the light. In some software packages, the artist can select the light object and then choose to treat that light as if it were the camera. The artist can tumble, dolly, or zoom the light the same way the artist would normally work with the camera. This is especially useful whenever a spotlight needs to be in a specific spot, like in a situation when the light needs to shine just past an object or the light's shadow needs to be shaped in a specific way to frame the scene. By using interactive placement, the artist is able to see through the light and control exactly where the light is illuminating. Then wherever the camera is looking is where the light is illuminating. In some software packages, the artist will even have the ability to see and control the edge and penumbra settings of the spotlight. This is not possible with all light types, but it can be a very effective method of light placement.

Isolating Lights

Even after the lights are created it is still the best workflow to continue isolating lights whenever tweaks are needed. Isolating lights allows in-progress render times to be reduced creating faster turnarounds. The artist will also need to remain in constant connection with how each light is influencing the scene and isolating lights allows that control. Losing sight of a light's contribution will cause the artist to lose control of the shot and the look of the final image.

Never Light over Black

While working and implementing all these workflows, the artist might find a situation where he or she is lighting one object or character over a black background. This is because only that object's lighting needs to be adjusted so everything else has been hidden and the subject in question can now be the focus. This is a great workflow for saving time, but aesthetically the lighting artist needs to be mindful and cautious to avoid lighting against a black background. Lighting over black can give an artist an inaccurate read of the character or object being lit especially in the darker tones around the edges. These dark edges will blend with the background and go unnoticed until the final image is pieced back together.

A solution to this problem is to light the character over a previously rendered still of the background. The still can either be loaded as a backdrop in the render view or as an image plane behind the character in the 3D environment. An image plane is just a single plane facing the camera with the image of the background applied as its texture. The plane is normally parented to the camera and always visible no matter where the camera is pointing. This way the artist can still benefit from the reduced render time while maintaining the visual integrity of the shot.

Saving Frames and Comparing Changes

Software packages are often able to cache or save rendered frames, allowing the artist to easily refer back to previous images. This is an incredibly useful tool since the ability to compare back to previous versions allows the lighter to see exactly what changed from the previous version and avoid any unexpected, unintended alterations to the look. The basic workflow when lighting is to render the frame, save that image, make one adjustment, re-render, see if the change is what was expected and repeat.

Isolating Problems through Exaggerated Values

At times it is necessary to identify which light is causing problems in the scene. Perhaps a light is casting a stray shadow or an undesired specular highlight. In a complex scene, it can be difficult to identify which light is causing the issue. A quick diagnostic method is to give lights exaggerated values to help identify the source of the problem. If the artist is trying to identify which light is causing a shadow across a character's face, he or she would select a few suspected lights and change their shadow color parameter to pure red, green, orange, blue, etc. In the subsequent render, if the problematic shadow appears red, the artist knows it was the light with the red shadow color. If none of the colors show up, more digging is required. This method can help save valuable time.

Figure 4.15 Exaggerating values can help the artist identify problematic areas and solve them more quickly.

Creating Wedges

A wedge is a tool that allows the artist to set up a series of frames where everything is identical except for one variable that is changed, rendered, and later analyzed. It is like running a science experiment on the shot. There is the single variable (the individual attribute being tested) and the control (everything else in the shot that remains the same.) The goal is to create a series of rendered frames the artist can go through frame by frame to determine which image looks the best and lock the value of that attribute to whatever the value was at that frame.

Animating the value of the intensity of a light is a simple wedge that can be run. The first thing to do is lock the animation so the render is working with a static pose. Then animate the value of the light between the minimum and maximum value reasonable given the scenario. Normally ten frames are enough to achieve a good breakdown and to find a suitable value.

A wedge can also be used when determining the position of a light. The most common wedge for positioning is to create a rotation wedge around the Y-axis. This can be done when first positioning the key light and will be easy to accomplish by following these steps:

1. Create a spotlight with the aiming point constrained to the character or focal point of the scene.
2. Place the spotlight the correct distance away and raise it to the pitch desired.
3. Reposition the axis point of the light to the same spot as the aim of the spotlight.
4. Set a key frame on the Y-rotation value on frame 1.

5. Move thirty-six frames ahead, and spin the light around the character or focal point by 360 degrees. Set another key frame. Now when the artist scrubs through those frames in between, the light should be circling the subject.

Render those frames and the artist will be able to see how the subject looks when the key light is in various positions (every 10 degrees) around the subject. Use this lighting test to determine the best key position for the shot. If the general key direction for

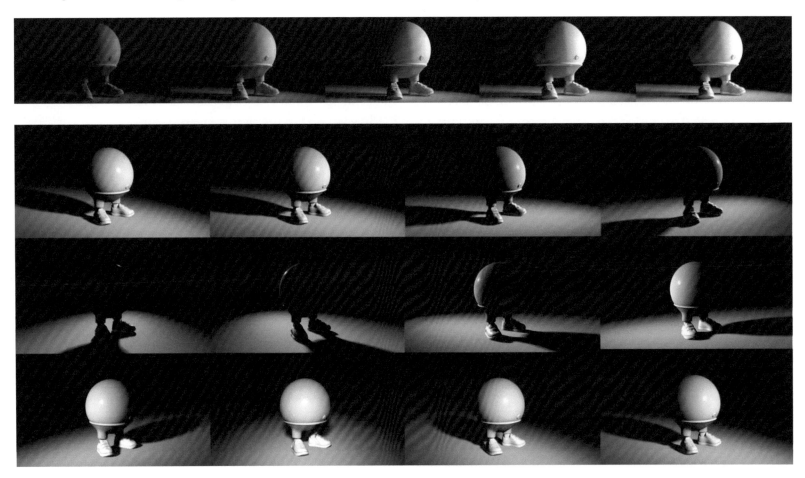

Figure 4.16 Wedges are a great way to analyze an image and make aesthetic decisions. Here is an example of both an intensity wedge (top) and a light rotation wedge (bottom).

the shot has been estimated by a color key, then the artist should focus the wedge on only that region.

Wedges are especially useful when working with a director, art director, or other supervisor. Normally these interactions end with the directors giving an abstract note such as making an object brighter or darker. By rendering a wedge of the brightness, the artist and the directors can go through the frames to come to a consensus of a concrete value that will work best for the scene.

Light Linking

In computer graphics, lighting artists have the ability to have certain lights influence only certain objects. This is known as light linking and can used in a variety of situations. Sometimes the character looks better with a key light in one position while the background looks better with the key light in a slightly different position. Other times there is a light that needs to shine through a wall or ceiling in order to properly simulate a bounce or fill light and illuminate the scene as accurately as possible.

Light linking can be very dangerous. If not used correctly, light linking can immediately make an image begin to look disjointed. Objects will not appear to interact correctly and a character could pass through a shadow in the environment and not get darker. It is therefore important for artists to understand that light linking should only be used when absolutely necessary. In some studios light linking controls have been taken away from the artists in a move designed to make the images more cohesive and structured more realistically.

Render Layers

Breaking a scene down into render layers is a big part of the lighter's job in many production situations. Render layers can be used to take a very large, complex scene that is difficult to render and break it down into smaller, more manageable chunks. They are also necessary for certain types of compositing procedures that may need to be done on a shot. Render layers can also increase work efficiency. Adjustments to the lighting of one element may only require one render layer to be redone instead of re-rendering the entire scene. Additionally, render layers give the artist increased control in postproduction.

Render layers do come with their negatives. Adding render layers certainly adds to the complexity of the scene and good organization must be utilized. If not done well, render layers can easily be combined incorrectly in the composite and cause false layering or other aesthetic mistakes. Also, more render layers means more storage necessary on the file system and more content management. All of these negatives can be overcome, but the artist must be trained, organized, and must understand the craft.

Setting Up Render Layers

There are several different methods of breaking shots out into render layers. Layers can be broken out based on objects. In this case the characters can be rendered separately from each other and the foreground of the set can be rendered separately from the background. Layers can also be broken out by individual components of the scene, where all the diffuse values, the specular values and the cast shadows have separate render layers.

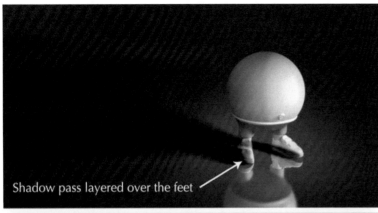

Shadow pass layered over the feet

Figure 4.17 Artists must take great care when assembling render layers to ensure they are working together properly.

There are countless combinations to the methodology of these breakouts. Certain studios have pipelines that must be followed while individuals also have their own preferences. Ultimately, as long as the artist is organized and mindful, any breakout of layers can be assembled into an aesthetically pleasing final image.

Beauty Render Layers

The first method of breaking renders into layers is by separating them into their own beauty passes. Beauty passes consist of each individual object or group of objects in the scene rendered separately. This includes individual render layers for the foreground, background, characters, and any other element in the scene worth separating.

Careful consideration must be taken into account whenever these layer breakouts occur. The artist cannot just cut elements out and paste them back together later without considering how they will work with one another. Doing so without great care may lead to layers looking segmented and separated from one another.

The first component to analyze is how these rendered elements interact with each other and influence one another. These interactions must be accounted for. For example, if the character is standing over the environment, does his or her shadow cast on the ground and surrounding elements? If so, that shadow must be taken into account in the environment layer. If the character were turned off completely, the background layers would be missing the shadow of the character cast on the floor.

This is achieved by having the character calculated into the background layer. The render settings are adjusted so the character itself is not visible but the cast shadow is. Each software package has a different way of handling these settings, but all should have the functionality to do so.

Conversely, the background would need to be accounted for in the character layer. Does the character's animation include the feet slightly penetrating the floor? If that is the case, the floor is held out of the character's render to account for this. This is often done by assigning a shader to the ground that will punch that area out of the character's alpha channel. Otherwise, the character will appear to be floating above the ground when the two images are pieced together.

Separating beauty layers can be extremely beneficial in post-production. When the artist wants to make adjustments isolated only to the characters, background, or other layers, he or she no longer is required to go back into the rendering software. These adjustments can quickly be made in the compositor and no re-renders are required, thus saving time.

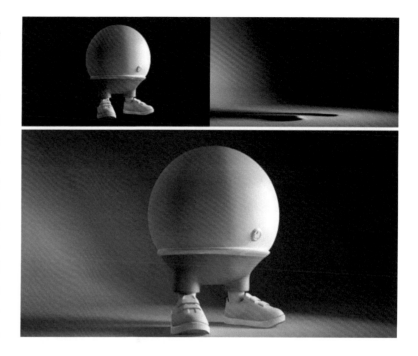

Figure 4.18 Example of beauty render layers.

Lighting Attribute Layers

Another way to break out render layers for a shot is to separate out the individual lighting attributes like diffuse, specular, and shadows. The main benefit of breaking these out into separate layers is to have more control over the detailed look of the shot. If more specularity is needed on a certain component, the artist can increase the value in the compositor as opposed to having to go back into the 3D scene, relighting, and doing a costly re-render. The artist could potentially waste an entire day waiting on a render that would have been unnecessary if he or she had broken the shot out as a separate lighting attribute layer.

Diffuse/Specular Layers

Diffuse and specular layers are very common lighting attribute layers. They are generally simple to set up and can give a huge amount of control. Creating a specular only or diffuse only pass can be done a few different ways. The first is to create a render layer where all the lights in that layer only emit either diffuse or specular light. The second is a similar method, but requires all the diffuse and specular values of the materials in the scene to be adjusted according to what layer is being rendered. Either way, the goal of the render is to have these two elements as separate components.

Shadow Passes

Shadow passes are another very common attribute layer. In the beauty layers section the shadows of the character were embedded into the background layer but the artist also has the option of working with shadows separately. To do this, all the objects in the scene receiving shadows should have their visibility turned on and all of their materials set to a flat, white lambert material. Any objects casting shadow are to be included in the scene with their normal materials applied, but their visibility turned off and set to cast shadows. This will result in an image that allows the user to isolate the shadowed areas and gives them the freedom to adjust the shadow contribution in postproduction if needed.

Figure 4.19 Example of diffuse and specular passes.

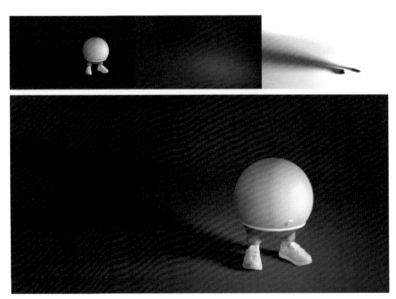

Figure 4.20 Example of beauty renders of the character and background with the shadow pass broken out separately.

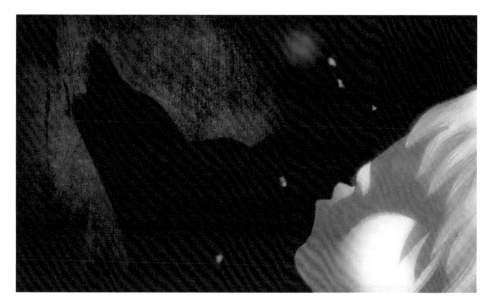

Figure 4.21 In this shot, the artist altered the shadow to showcase the character's inner animal. Image from the animated film *Feral,* property of Daniel Sousa.

Other than allowing for greater aesthetic control, shadow passes could provide an opportunity to save on render time. If the camera for the scene is locked off and the environment being rendered is stationary, the artist can choose to render only a single frame of the background and then apply the shadow pass of the animated character to give it all the elements needed. The character pass then can be layered on top, finishing the shot. By not rendering every frame of the background for the entire shot, a significant amount of time can be saved.

Shadow passes also allow the opportunity to have greater control over silhouettes and shadows that are the center of interest for a given shot. For example, situations arise when the artist would want to have greater control of the shadow in the compositor in order to distort the shape or modify it in some way. It is also possible for the shadow pass to be from a completely different version of the character and applied to the scene if the story calls for that. This second version of the character could be behaving completely differently as a storytelling point in an animated film.

Specialty Layers

In CG lighting, there are other layers that are prevalent but do not necessarily coincide with specific lighting attributes. These layers are common to the lighter's workflow and should be treated with the same care.

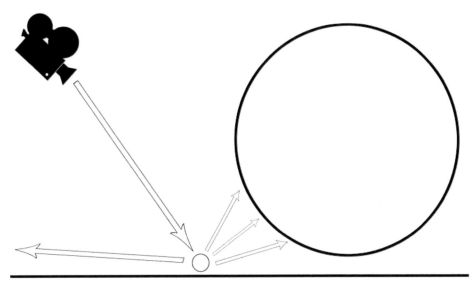

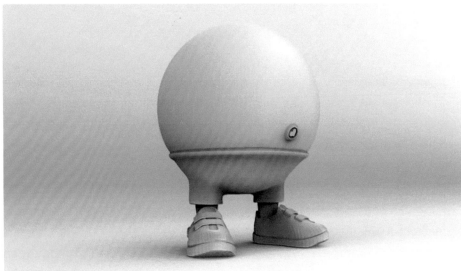

Figure 4.22 An ambient occlusion render is one that calculates the proximity from one object to the next and displays the results with a visual representation of values from 0 to 1, or black to white.

Ambient Occlusion

Ambient occlusion is a layer available in most render packages. An ambient occlusion render is one that calculates the proximity from one object to the next and displays the results with a visual representation of values from 0 to 1, or black to white. In other words, ambient occlusion, or AO for short, calculates how many points on a surface are occluded from light by other objects in a scene. Normally, this can be achieved by applying specialty shaders to the objects in the scene. These values are determined from rays that are fired into the scene looking to hit an object. Once they hit that object, they reflect off and see how long it takes to hit another bit of geometry. The nearer those two objects are, the darker the resulting visual image is. The greater the distance it takes that bouncing ray to hit another object, the closer to white the image becomes.

In the composite, this image can be used in a couple of ways. The most common is to simulate the contact shadow where two objects meet. This is normally done by multiplying the ambient occlusion pass by the beauty render. This will allow the darker parts of the ambient occlusion render to darken the appropriate areas of the beauty render. Additionally, ambient occlusion renders can be given color to simulate a stronger bounce value between two objects. More will be discussed about integrating ambient occlusion passes in later chapters.

The setting most used to fine tune ambient occlusion shaders is the spread angle. This is the angle the ray takes after hitting the initial surface. The spread angle will control how hard or soft to make the ambient occlusion render look. The artist will normally change the spread angle to allow the look to echo reflective qualities of materials.

Ambient occlusion renders also have a tendency to be noisy and grainy. This is a result of too few rays being fired into the scene. In most cases, the ambient occlusion shader gives the artist the option of increasing the number of rays, but be careful as it can dramatically escalate render times.

Reflection Passes

Reflections are an element that will often need to be controlled independently. This comes up in a variety of circumstances. Often it is just a simple reflection in a mirror, a window, or in a character's eye. The artist will often want to control these reflections on his or her own since reflections often need to be fine tuned to meet an aesthetic goal. The result is a reflection pass that can be composited in later.

The best way to set up a reflection layer is to first turn off reflections in the original render. Then the material for the reflective element will need to be set up

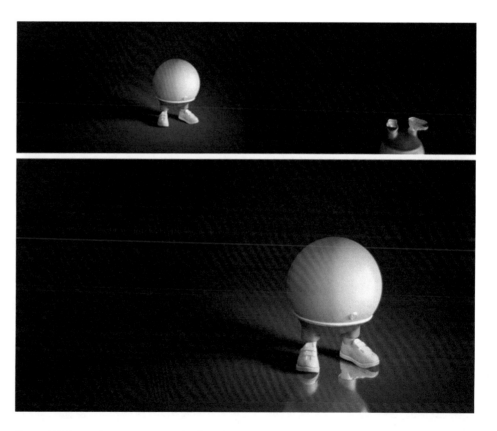

Figure 4.23 By creating a separate pass for the reflections the artist is able to quickly adjust their contribution to the final image.

in a way to allow for pure reflections with the accurate amount of reflective blur applied. The reflection contribution can always be toned down in the post process if a pure reflection is too strong. To obtain a pure reflection, the object must be given a material that can calculate the reflective surface. A blinn shader is often the easiest and most straightforward way of approaching this. The settings are as follows:

Now the reflective object will have a pure reflection assigned to it. The artist must be sure to stay consistent with the material attributes to the original object. For example if there is a bump map or spec matte associated with the object, it should also have those attributes in the reflection pass. For some reflection passes to feel convincing, an artist may need to render a facing ratio pass to compensate for the fact that different materials reflect different amounts based on a viewed angle. The final step is to add the desired surrounding lights and geometry to be reflected and rendered.

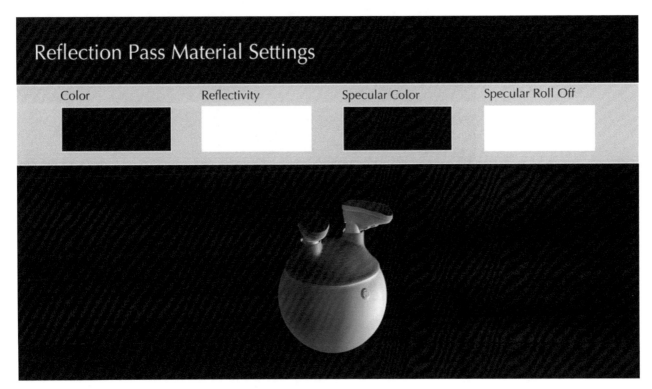

Figure 4.24 A reflection pass can be created by using a blinn shader with these settings.

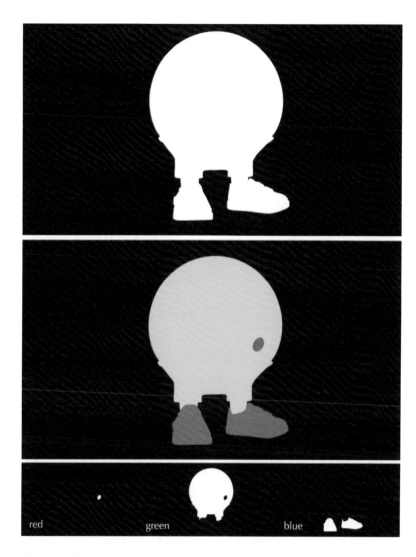

Figure 4.25 Mattes and RGB mattes are an excellent way to isolate areas of the render for adjustments in postproduction.

Matte/RGB Matte Layers

A valuable and inexpensive render layer that will give the artist additional control in the composite is the matte pass. Matte passes are a way to isolate the alpha channel of a particular object or section of an object with the intention of tweaking it in postproduction. An example might be to create a matte layer for the shirt of a particular character with the plan of slightly shifting its color in the composite. This method is incredibly useful when trying to make minor tweaks while trying to avoid a re-render of the entire shot. Since matte passes normally only need isolated elements and usually lighting isn't required, the render times are much, much faster.

The easiest way to set one up is to use a simple shader that does not have reflectivity or specularity. Assign that material only to the object to be isolated. The only other objects calculated are those that come between that object and the camera. For those, just assign a shader that will punch out the alpha (black hole) along with no reflection or specularity either. Then, once in the composite, the alpha channel generated in this render can be used to make the necessary adjustments.

For greater control over more elements in the shot, artists will often create RGB matte layers in order to handle up to three different mattes in one render. Instead of applying a white surface shader (or similar) material to the objects, the artist will apply either a pure red (1 0 0), green (0 1 0), or blue color (0 0 1). Then, once in the compositor, each one of these matte layers can be isolated by pulling an alpha from only the red, green, or blue color channels of the image. This method will reduce render times even further by limiting the renders to one RGB pass instead of three regular matte passes and give the artist more control over the final image. Implementing matte passes is discussed further in later chapters.

RGB Light Layers

Lighting properties can be controlled in much the same way as an RGB matte layer. The lights within the scene can be altered to emit either pure red, green, or blue light. The resulting image can be controlled identically to the RGB matte pass except this time they control the areas of the image each light is influencing. Additionally, the lights can be broken down even further into their diffuse and specular values. RGB lights can isolate just these components to be controlled independently as well. This will ultimately give the artists even more control in the postproduction process. This method can be beneficial, especially when time is pressing and additionally, like RGB mattes, the artist can save render time and file storage by controlling three separate elements with one render.

Shadows are another element that can be broken down into RGB elements and either controlled or applied in the comp. The layer would be set up the same way as the normal render layer, but the shadow pass will be altered so the shadow color is a pure red, green, or blue.

Ultimately, there are an infinite number of render layers that can be created. The methodologies in this section should be viewed as general guidelines to some of the most popular ones, but certainly not hardened rules. RGB mattes and light attribute layers, for example, can actually be run as subcomponents of shaders through buffers or AOVs rather than render layers in some software packages. There are layers that will be shot specific and will not fall into one of these norms. The only limitation is the creativity of the artist to construct a way to control the different elements of the scene.

All that being said, it is important to note that in most situations more is not better. Just because an artist has the ability to break out each element separately, it is not always the best method. More render layers can mean more complexity that could lead to a disjointed final image if not controlled skillfully. The artist must always be sure to be mindful when deciding what layers need to be broken out. By harnessing this ability, the artist will gain ultimate control and focus solely on building the look he or she wants.

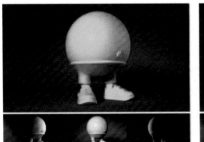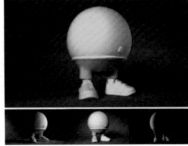

Figure 4.26 The same principle for isolating RGB channels can be applied to beauty, diffuse, specular, reflection, and many other passes. In these example images the rendered image is above with each red, green, and blue channel isolated in the image below.

Render Workflow

As a lighter, rendering is a crucial part of the job. Whether it is generating quick test renders or running high resolution beauty frames for a giant billboard, understanding and utilizing the ins and outs of this process is mandatory.

Image File Types

Part of rendering an image is determining the file type. This file type can have a huge impact on the size of the file being generated and the overall quality. There are different file types that can be used and they each have their advantages and disadvantages.

JPEG

JPEG images are compressed images designed to give decent image quality within a small file size. JPEGs are generally used for posting on the Internet, sending through emails, or any other time a smaller file size is required. This smaller file size comes with a price. The amount of compression is substantial and can cause artifacts in the image. This is simply because getting the smaller file means dropping information from the image which can lead to a loss of detail causing visual problems. JPEGs are great in many situations but should never be used when delivering a final image.

TIFF or TARGA

When making the leap from test renders to final images, the artist wants to move into "lossless" file formats like TIFFs or TARGAs. These formats are referred to as lossless since they do not lose data when being saved, which is different than "lossy" formats like JPEGs, which compress the image. While these formats are larger file sizes, they also contain the maximum amount of image information possible and are therefore more versatile once the image is being composited. TIFFs generally are more common than TARGAs since they are compatible with more programs that are generally used more frequently.

OpenEXR

OpenEXR is a high dynamic range file format created by Industrial Light and Magic specifically for computer graphics. These files can save either as lossless or lossy images. More impressively, Open-EXR files have the capability to store more data than just the RGBA channels of a normal image. They have the capacity to store many render layers and/or right and left eye stereo frames in one image file. This capability makes OpenEXR files very attractive to high end companies and has become more and more common since its release in 2003.

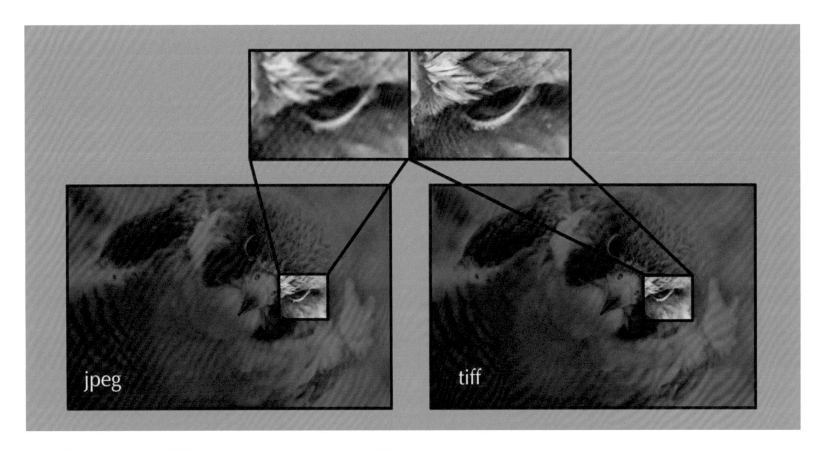

Figure 4.27 Upon closer inspection, JPEG images can appear much lower resolution than TIFFs.

Bit Depth

Another render setting to consider is bit depth. Bit depth refers to the number of memory bits devoted to storing each pixel of an image's color information. The greater the bit depth, the more color data the image has to handle finer gradations. Generally speaking, images are normally stored at 8-, 16-, or 32-bit color depths depending on the need; 32-bit images are known as floating point images because of their ability to save seemingly countless numbers of colors and also have the ability to store white values above 1.

Generally speaking, 8-bit images are a decent render quality, but will contain some banding and image artifacting; 16-bit images are usually free of banding and, visually speaking, have a continuing uninterrupted tone; 32-bit or floating-point images are commonly used because of their ability to store the most data and a high dynamic range. Obviously, file size will increase as bit depth goes up and images become more complex.

Render Quality

Image quality and compression are not the only things that can cause artifacts in an image. These artifacts include the common CG problems of aliasing (stair-stepping) and noise (or chatter). Depending on the renderer, render quality is a blanket term that will center on the number of samples used during the render. They are often termed something like "low, medium, and high" or "draft and production." The lower settings are meant for work-in-progress tests while the higher settings are intended for final images. Renderers will often default to these lower settings assuming the artist will initially be testing the image in the renderer. Increasing these render quality settings can greatly increase render times since more calculations are necessary but can also greatly improve image quality.

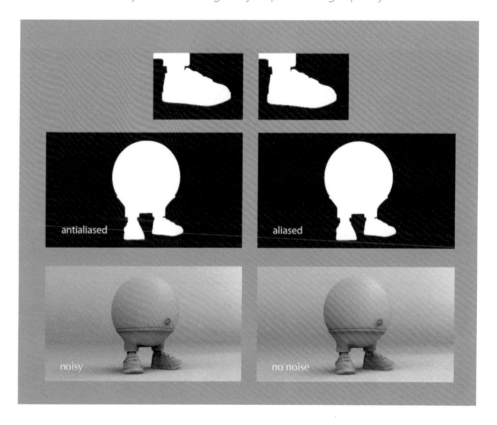

Figure 4.28 Aliased edges and render "noise" are common problems in CG renders that must be addressed.

Image Outputting Structure

Once the image and file settings are in place, it is time to set up a structure to organize the outputting images. This is a crucial step that often gets overlooked by artists first starting out. By creating an organized structure for outputting the images, the artist always knows where the rendered images are being stored and can access them quickly and easily. This will save hours of time later when trying to find old frames or re-rendering images already created but lost in the mass.

Each artist or project has their own structure and naming convention. These naming conventions must be followed exactly, especially on collaborative projects, so all participants are on the same page. Generally speaking, these conventions include having an image folder for each shot and subfolders for each rendered layer and their corresponding z-depth render or other secondary image frames. Then, within those directories, the individual image files live with their own naming convention, usually something like the name of the render layer and the frame number. It is important to pad the frame numbers so they will always play in sequence regardless of the software being used to process the images.

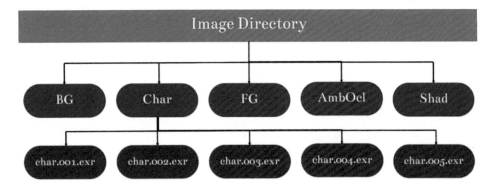

Figure 4.29 By creating an organized image file structure the artist can save lots of time and headaches in the long run.

Many software packages and renderers allow the artist to automate these output settings through variables like "%f" or "%l" to designate the current frame or layer being rendered.

Overnight Render Settings and Tricks

There are additional tricks and techniques that can be used during work-in-progress renders that can speed up one's workflow. The obvious one is just to reduce the resolution and image size. As previously mentioned with work-in-progress lighting renders, it is common for daily renders to be around 33–50 percent the total size of the final. This generally leaves enough data to be viewed and analyzed while allowing the rendered frames to complete overnight.

The second method is intended to aid longer shots. Often, animated shots can be quite long and last for twenty to thirty seconds or several hundred frames. These shots can be driven by dialogue so the characters are in a fixed position. It is therefore possible to only render every second, fourth, eighth, or even tenth frame depending on how slow and how long the shot is. By rendering incremental frames in this way, the artist can significantly increase overnight render efficiency and overall quality of the work while still being able to analyze samples of the entire shot.

During production, there are also little tests the artist can complete to ensure there are no problems when a shot is sent to final render. This includes running a segment of frames (usually five to ten frames) with the final render settings to verify that the final image will look as expected. Additionally, the artist can choose to run those frames with various render settings which will determine the best look with the most efficient render times. By doing this, the artist is hopefully able to identify any problems early on so there isn't a panic as the deadline approaches.

Final Render Settings and Tricks

The first thing that must be done when preparing the shot for final render is to enable motion blur (if it is being used in the shot) and to increase all the anti-alias and sample settings to final render quality. These settings will be tweaked based on the project requirements since often projects with very tight schedules will choose to bypass motion blur because the additional render time is too much to absorb. Once these settings are determined, the final renders are launched and the shot is done, right? Unfortunately, this is rarely the case.

Despite the fact that testing has occurred, it is almost inevitable that render artifacts will emerge. A major problem in animated projects is the noise and chatter. This book has addressed this previously but there is another way of tackling this problem other than increasing the render quality. In many cases, the best way to solve a noisy scene is to render it at a higher image size and then scale it down in postproduction. This increased size will create more data and ultimately less noise once the image is scaled back down. Also, if only a small segment of the screen is problematic, some renderers give the artist the option of only rendering a small section of the frame. In this case, the artist can render that section at a higher resolution, scale it down, and layer it over the original in postproduction to eliminate the illusion of chatter.

There are countless other adjustments to render settings that can be made on a per shot or per show basis. If the background is exceptionally noisy but the camera doesn't move, is it possible to only render a still frame and use that for the duration of the shot? Is it a 2D camera move that can be tracked in postproduction so only one frame of the background can be rendered? Can certain objects have lower render qualities and still appear the same visually? There may be objects that are either highly motion blurred, too far from the camera, or too out of focus to see clearly so reducing their render size could help. These are the types of questions lighters must learn to ask during the final render process to make it go as smoothly and efficiently as possible.

Final Thoughts

Ultimately, each artist develops his or her own system for working through an animated project. But with some pre-planning and attention to detail, the artist can work efficiently, save precious time, and eliminate much of the stress associated with being disorganized and unknowing. Following this type of workflow will make an artist better, faster, and much happier.

Interview
with Michael Knapp

Art Director :: Blue Sky Studios.

Q. What is your current job/role at your company?
A. I am an Art Director at Blue Sky Studios. My background is in illustration, storyboarding, set and character design, as well as color theory. I've been art directing at Blue Sky for the last nine years.

Q. What inspired you to work in this industry?
A. Even as an illustrator, I was always inspired as much by film composition and lighting as I was fine art and illustration. I've always been fascinated by the marriage of art and technology, so when the opportunity presented itself to design on Blue Sky's Robots I jumped at the chance. It became clear to me very quickly that this medium was a perfect fit for my sensibilities. I love the process and the collaborative nature of filmmaking (which was very refreshing after seven years of freelancing as an illustrator in solitude).

Q. What non-CG artwork inspires you?
A. Lately, I've been really inspired by the work of Cartoon Saloon—first by *Secret of Kells* and more recently by the gorgeous and charming *Song of the Sea*. The graphic motifs, the designs and intricate compositions … The beautiful use of textures and shapes. It all appeals to what drew me to illustration and animation in the first place. I find a lot of inspiration in European comics, children's books, graphic novels, and experiments in sequential art narratives such the work of Brian Selznick or Shaun Tan. My friends and co-workers constantly inspire me with their personal projects—one of the perks of working at a studio like Blue Sky is being surrounded by such strong and varied talent. Movies have always been a great source of inspiration for me—especially the old Ridley Scott and Spielberg films from the 70s and 80s, and then animated classics like *The Secret of Nimh*, *Sleeping Beauty* and *The Iron Giant*.

Q. Can you give us an idea of what your process is when you are designing a color key for a sequence? In other words, how do you take a scene that is meant to be dramatic or emotional and translate that to visuals?

A. There are a lot of factors involved in planning color keys for a sequence: time of day, weather conditions in the scene, the emotional content or theme of the scene … It all starts from the story and what the scene is trying to convey. How are the characters feeling? Do they feel alone in their situation? How do we as storytellers want the audience to feel? Do we want them to feel like they're in the scene with the characters? Or is the shot more objective, and are we trying to put some distance between the audience and the characters?

The answers to these questions (and many more) help determine whether a shot is backlit, beauty-lit, front three-quarter lit, diffusely lit to create atmosphere … Bouncing soft warm light into the face of a character can romanticize a shot. Harsh top light can make the character feel oppressed in the scene. Is the character's intent clear, thus calling for direct lighting on the face with a clear view of their eyes? Or are they hiding something that would call for us to throw shadow across their face? Will the character read as a light shape over a dark background? Or vice versa? If the scene is emotionally intense, we may use a lot of contrast in the scene. We might use a limited value range if we're trying to convey a specific mood.

There are a lot of possibilities for any scenario and no absolute right answers, but part of my job as art director is working closely with the directors to get a good feeling for the "pulse" of the film and making my creative choices based on that. There might be sequences in multiple films that I work on that might be familiar to one another, but I'll make completely different decisions based on what comes before them and what happens after.

In terms of the nuts and bolts of designing a color key, we start as simply as possible—basic figure/ground relationship between the character and background. What is the main source of light in the scene? Is there anything in the story which dictates the light direction or a light source? What direction is the key light coming from and does that direction work for all the shots in a sequence? If it's an exterior, how does the sky light affect the scene? If it's an interior, are there direct light sources in the environment or diffuse light sources? The set design really dictates how we will light the scene, so planning ahead is critical. If we want dappled light to set a peaceful mood for a forest scene, we need enough trees to motivate that treatment. If the scene takes place in an interior setting, we need practical light sources to help us feature our characters.

Once the basics in a color key are solid, then we can start looking at whether we need to use a rim light. Do we need any volumetrics? How much atmosphere or dust in the air is present? How will we use depth of field?

We plan color keys thinking about how all the shots flow together as an entire sequence rather than a series of shots. This forces us to think about one main idea for the lighting setup in a scene, and then if we need to deviate from that setup for a specific shot we'll find ways to do it without it jarring the audience.

Q. Can you tell us some of the techniques you use to get the audience to focus on the character or main action of the sequence?

A. This really begins with the set design and set dressing. We design and arrange our sets so that even when the characters aren't there, your eye wants to go to the right place. The character becomes the final piece to the puzzle of any given composition. When it feels appropriate, we create a pool of light in the scene where the characters will be staged. If this feels too manufactured, we might use the ground material to vignette the focal area of a shot instead (some well-placed moss can be very helpful in a case like this). We use set dressing elements (trees, rocks, furniture …) to help guide your eye to the right place either by balancing out a composition or by framing the subject of the shot.

Q. Is there one sequence or project that you are particularly proud of?

A. One of the most challenging and satisfying sequences I've worked on was the pod patch sequence in *Epic*. We had to transform one location from an idyllic pond to a frantic battleground, build the set and plan the lighting to work from any angle, whether on the water's surface or up in the trees looking down, and slowly evolve the lighting from majestic dappled sunlight to stormy skies over the course of over eight minutes of film. All this while populating the scene with hundreds if not thousands of characters who (by design) blended in with their natural surroundings. It was some of the hardest and most gratifying work on any film I've worked on.

Q. If you could tell yourself one piece of advice when you were first starting out in this industry, what would it be?

A. It's funny—I never actively pursued a career in animation. An opportunity presented itself and I thought it seemed like a good idea at the time (that was fifteen years ago!). I thought I was going to be an illustrator all my life, so I'm not sure any advice would have done me a whole lot of good early on. That said, here's something I wish I had learned earlier—it would have saved me a lot of grief:

Don't buy into the idea that anyone has everything figured out. Making these films is an incredibly complex undertaking, and no one place has a perfect process. Always look for ways to do things better and smarter and learn to trust your fellow artists. I think this applies to both the technical and the creative aspects of making CG films.

Q. In your opinion, what are some of the things you would say make a successful lighting artist?

A. Needless to say, there's a technical threshold that must be met by any successful lighting artist, but from my non-technical point of view, here are a few things that I've found to be important:

First and foremost, the ability to break a shot down into its simplest form and make it structurally sound. A lot of lighting (and traditional) artists get caught up in the details early and might create a shot or image with a lot of pretty things in it, but it will be fundamentally flawed. Once the shot works in its simplest form, then the bells and whistles will make it that much more successful.

The successful lighting artists I've worked with have fantastic observational skills and notice the little things that make an image convincing: the way light blooms at the edge of frame, the reflected light cast by a brushed metal surface, where to let the focus soften in a shot so it isn't perfectly CG crisp, etc. In our films, realism isn't necessarily the goal. I prefer the term "naturalism." If the shot looks and feels right while conveying the emotional tone of the sequence, that can be more convincing than pure realism. This goes hand in hand with understanding visual storytelling and having a strong sense of what details help tell the story and which ones distract from it.

I also think that the most successful artists (of any collaborative medium) are good communicators and learn to interpret creative notes in ways that capture their intent and spirit, not just their literal aspects. Communication is also key in figuring out the aesthetic tastes of the person giving the notes (which can be incredibly helpful).

Still from the animated short *Edmond était un âne (Edmond was a Donkey)*.
Property of Papy3d/ONF NFB/ARTE.

5

Dissecting a Well-lit Shot

Now that this book has discussed both the technical elements and the workflow of the lighter, it is time to dedicate the rest of the book to the artistic side of lighting. Training the lighter's artistic eye by understanding what makes a well-lit shot is the most important element to being a lighter. Knowing the technical information and workflow will only get an artist so far. It is this artistic understanding and implementation of those skills that elevates one lighter above the rest.

New lighters have a tendency to jump head first into producing their own work. While it is certainly important to get in there and start lighting, it is also absolutely necessary to take the time to observe and learn the craft by observing the work of others. It is through this study that an artist begins to understand the components of a well-lit shot and how those concepts can be utilized in his or her own work.

What are the Elements of a Well-lit Shot?

As mentioned earlier, a successful shot has three major elements. First and foremost, it needs to help tell the story by setting the mood through the use of light. Second, it should direct the viewer's eye with subtle techniques to control the audience's gaze. Last, a well-lit shot should always create good visual shaping. These topics were touched upon in Chapter 1, but this chapter will delve deeper and break these elements down further.

Telling the Story by Emphasizing the Mood

A necessary component for any successful storyteller is the ability to set the appropriate mood for the audience. By inducing a particular feeling or state of mind, the storyteller is setting the proper stage for the actions to follow. In animation, all artists are storytellers regardless of their job title. Lighters have the particular job of helping tell the story through color, contrast, saturation, and all the other visual components that make up an image. This section will explore a variety of ways these visual elements can be implemented to successfully set the mood.

Light Placement and Intensity in Relation to Mood

The placement of lights and their relative intensities is a huge factor in the creation of mood. Lights can be positioned either to enhance a character's beauty or conversely to make that same character appear malicious. The relative intensities of the lights determine the overall contrast level of the scene. A high contrast scene has a very different mood from a lower contrast scene. These lighting decisions will help lay the groundwork for the story to come.

High Key

A common lighting practice in classic Hollywood musicals and comedies was high key lighting. In high key lighting situations the key light and fill light are more frontal and given similar intensity values. The ultimate goal of this style is

Figure 5.1 Examples of high key lighting. Still from the animated short *El Vendedor de Humo*, property of Primer Focus and produced by Carlos Escutia.

to minimize shadows, especially harsh shadows, that could disrupt and distract from the overall soft, gentle look desired. The frontal nature also flattens out smaller details so this lighting practice is much more focused on the larger details and overall form of the characters and objects.

Low Key

Low key lighting is the exact opposite situation. Fill values are dropped and key positions are rotated further around the subjects, creating longer, harsher shadows. The overall look is much more dramatic with a grittier, moodier aesthetic. This style is appropriate for a villain and any scene where mystery and suspense are present.

Under-lighting

Under-lighting is also a light rig generally used to portray evil characters and ominous scenes. It is when the key is positioned beneath the character, causing long upward shadows.

This is a very unnatural feeling lighting scenario because it rarely happens in nature. The sun and moon are constantly above the horizon line so seeing this light feels eerie. Only in situations with manmade light like campfires or low-placed light bulbs will there be a situation like this in the world.

Figure 5.2 Examples of low key lighting. Still from the animated short *Leucotopia*, property of Mehdi Louala, Geoffrey Godet, Nicolas Lejeune, Céline Hermann, and Simon Legrand. **Produced by Supinfocom (right).**

Figure 5.3 Examples of under-lighting. Still from the animated short *Little Freak*. Property of Edwin Schaap **(right).**

Rim Key

Lighting with a strong key that outlines the character from behind is another technique for light placement. This technique creates a strong "rim key" and is useful in three main situations. The first is when the lighting scenario calls for it. This normally occurs when the character is standing between the camera and something very bright like a sunset. Usually this would mean the character is silhouetted with a bright rim to integrate with the surroundings.

Another situation is if the characters are very small on the screen and the audience needs to be aware of their presence. A key rim can help pop that character out of the background and make the viewers focus their attention on the character without realizing it. Obviously the lighting situation would need to be respected, but this can still be achieved in most instances.

The third major situation is when the silhouette of the character needs to pop because of a specific hand gesture or body position. By positioning the key light behind the character, the artist can emphasize the silhouette which can aid in the storytelling. Most often this is when a character is pointing or making some sort of other hand gesture and it is difficult to read the fingers.

Figure 5.4 Examples of rim key lighting. Images from *Marilyn Myller*, used courtesy of Mikey Please.

Shadow

Light placement not only benefits the illumination but can also aid in shadow casting as a tool for storytelling. A properly positioned shadow can create a dark swath in the image that can be utilized in a variety of fashions. Sometimes the scene will involve two characters that are in dispute and it is beneficial to show a visual divide between the two. The lighter may choose to construct the rig so a bold shadow is cast between the characters.

Shadows that harshly slash across the character are normally avoided when attempting to make a character look more beautiful. In some situations, however, this may not be the objective. There may be a battle or a chase sequence that is filled with drama. The hero may fear for his or her life and that tension needs to be felt by the viewing audience. That drama may best be emphasized further with sharp, angling shadows on the faces of the characters in order to truly emphasize the gravity of the situation.

The timing of passing shadows can become very important in storytelling if the character is moving through space. When traveling in a park or forest, the character will pass through patches of light and shadow as a result of sun breaking through the canopy of overhead trees. If the scene depicts two children playing and running around a shaded playground, then the timing of those patches of light and shadow will be nice and evenly spaced and potentially a little slower than they would happen in reality. If a monster suddenly pops out and starts chasing the children, the timing of shadow and light patches could increase in speed. This would showcase the drama of the moment and make the characters feel like they are traveling at a faster speed than before. As the monster closes in, the speed can increase even more to continue to build the tension. But a hero jumps in and saves the day, allowing the pacing to return to normal. This is just one of countless examples of how shadow placement is a powerful tool in storytelling.

Figure 5.5 In both of these examples the shadow is designed to help frame the character. Still from the animated short *Shave It*. Property of 3DAR.

Color and Mood

Lighting for the purpose of establishing mood and telling a story must include a study into color and its effect on the audience. Previously, this book discussed how subtle pinks and warm tones can make a scene feel inviting and even romantic. Although these color associations are something that may seem fairly obvious when discussed, the audience does not often perceive these color shifts. An argument could be made that color alone is the most salient feature of animated films. Color has a strong, deep-rooted place in the human brain and an artist can utilize those associations in order to subtly create mood.

Color is not only an integral part of how the audience interacts with film, but also how humans interact with the world. The study of color and its influence on mood is inexact. No one color gives every person the same emotion every time. A soft blue like the sky can be calming and soothing, but when someone is unhappy it can be said that they "feel blue." Red can mean fire, passion, love, and action, but at the same time symbolize warmth and comfort.

There are two general ways that a viewer can interpret color: biologically and culturally. Biologically speaking there are colors in nature like green for foliage, blue for water, and orange for fire. Each one of these is thought to have a deep-seated impact on the way humans view color. They are universal and timeless and are unchangeable in the human psyche.

One interesting example is the biological influence the color blue can have on appetite. This is thought to be because there are very few blue colored foods in nature. There are no blue leafy vegetables or blue meats. This unnaturalness of blue food actually is thought to trigger the part of the

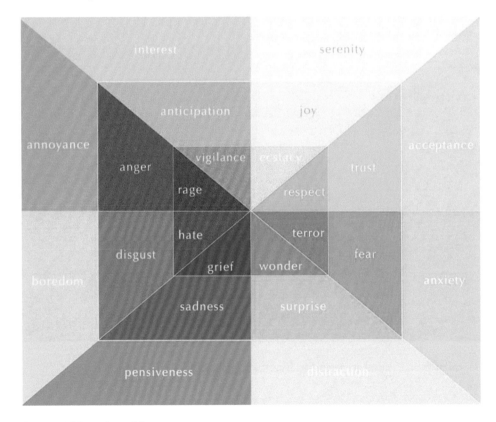

Figure 5.6 Color and mood chart.

brain that cautions people against eating it since it is perceived as strange and possibly poisonous. Many weight loss specialists will even make the claim that eating off a blue plate will cause patients to lose more weight. Stronger still, they claim that by simply adding blue food coloring to dishes like pasta, one can actually minimize the craving for certain foods at certain times.

Warm, reddish tones have exactly the opposite effect. Reds will increase heart rate and increase appetite. Tomatoes, apples, raw meat, pomegranates, raspberries and strawberries all exist in nature and therefore we are much more comfortable associating reds with food. Think of corporate logos like McDonald's, Wendy's, and Pizza Hut. All of these logos have the advantage of raising heart rates and have the added benefit of attracting attention.

Translate these examples into the world of CG lighting. There may be a scene where a child is forced to eat a plate of unwanted vegetables when, really, she wants the big piece of cake sitting in the middle of the table. It would be wise of the lighting artist to have the unwanted food in cool light while the cake just so happens to fall into the warm appetizing light.

Cultural bias toward color varies from society to society. The colors of flags, money, and sports teams can greatly influence an individual's reaction. For Americans, green is the color of money, but in Islam it symbolizes the heavens. Purple, referred to as Tyrian purple in ancient Rome, was the color of royalty and wealth. While a lovely color, Tyrian purple was a symbol of grandeur because purple dye was extremely expensive to obtain. The process involved craftsmen gathering thousands of marine snails and boiling them with special chemicals just to get a few drops. In modern times, purple does not have this association since its rarity is no longer the case. Therefore, these types of color associations are ones that are not inherent in people but are dictated by an individual's specific surroundings.

This is just one minor example of the influence of color on mood in a CG scene. There are countless ways color can impact the audience's reaction to a scene depending on the situation and there are several examples at the end of this section. Each scene and each shot is unique and must be handled independently and with care in order to achieve the maximum impact.

Figure 5.7 Blue food is perceived as far less appetizing than warmer colored foods.

Figure 5.8 This distinct pink color is only used in this film when the potion is present. © Disney.

Figure 5.9 Contrast defines the value difference between the brightest and darkest points in terms of luminance and/or color.

Symbolic Color in Films

Certain colors can come to represent specific emotions, elements, or even characters in films. It is not uncommon in a film to assign a certain palette or color temperature for given situations. Art designs can even call for all the hero characters to have warm, red tones while villains are represented by blue, cool tones. Or perhaps every time there are strong, warm colors the scene is full of danger. Green tones may repeatedly be present when there is hope and life in a certain environment, while the inclusion of a blue color could only appear whenever a certain character is around.

One great example of this is from Disney's *Emperor's New Groove*. In this film there is a potion that plays a key role in the film's plot. That potion is a bright pink color and that pink color is only present in the film when the potion is around. That pink color is a direct representative of that story point. In fact, the introduction of the potion is set up by a series of cool toned shots that seem to have all warmth sucked out of them. Then, when the potion finally appears on screen, the color visually jumps off the screen into the audience's lap because the withholding of warm tones made this vibrant pink's impact even more powerful.

Contrast and Saturation

When discussing color and light one must also discuss contrast and saturation as well. Contrast defines the value difference between the brightest and darkest points in terms of luminance and/or color.

If an image is said to have high contrast, it means the difference between the brightest point and darkest point is drastic. Alternatively if a shot has low contrast, the brightest and darkest points are not as far apart from one another.

Contrast levels definitely influence mood. High contrast images almost completely define an entire genre in the history of American cinema known as Film Noir. Film Noir, or "Black Films," get their name because not only are they about grim subjects but the films themselves are visually dark and carry heavy black values. These graphic images depict a gloomy world filled with murder, betrayal, and an overall somber outlook. When lighting a scene that is meant to be full of tension and anxiety, one would most likely approach it with high contrast lighting.

Low contrast images have a much softer and more inviting feel. The brightest areas are tamped down a bit and the shadows and dark points are lifted slightly with a lot of midtone values. If lighting a romantic or comedic scene then the softness of low contrast lighting would probably be the best choice.

Saturation refers to how vivid the color appears. Saturated colors are more pure than unsaturated ones, meaning their value in one or more of the three RGB settings approaches a 100 percent contribution. High levels of saturation generally cause colors to pop off the screen more dramatically.

Generally speaking, more saturation is used on happier sequences or on a bright, sunny day while less saturation is used in more dreary scenarios. In an Internet search for "sad images," it will be immediately noticed that the resulting images are predominantly desaturated. Do the same search for "happy images" and all the images are full of more vibrant colors.

Figure 5.10a *Giant* © Sanford Roth / A.M.P.A.S. / mptvimages.com.

Figure 5.10b *Doris Day* © Martin Mills / mptvimages.com.

Figure 5.11 Generally speaking, more vibrant, colorful images are thought of as being happy versus black and white or low saturation images that are viewed as sad.

Directing the Viewer's Eye

As discussed in Chapter 1, directing the viewer's eye is a key part of the lighter's job. This section will build upon those earlier concepts and explore new ways the artist can modify a scene to manipulate the viewer's focus onto the essential story point.

What Draws the Eye When a Viewer Looks at a Screen?

There is a trick artists can use when looking at an image to help determine the focal point. It involves looking at a blurred version of the image to help minimize the shapes and objects and just evaluate the overall tones. Audiences are often drawn to the brightest or most contrasted section of the image and those areas are made apparent in this simplified, blurred version. An artist can artificially blur an image in an image manipulation software but the easiest way to accomplish this is to just squint. Squinting to analyze the image is a trick from painting and photography and is used for the same purpose. This will mush the image into a series of general shapes and allow the artist to make aesthetic decisions based on simple composition principles.

Leading Lines with Light

Using leading lines to draw the viewer's eye to the subject matter is a common design technique. Normally, it is discussed in regard to elements within the scene forming a visual line that leads the viewer's eye to the subject, but this is absolutely true in lighting as well. The artist could structure a shot in such a way that the light and shadow will actually create a path for the viewer to follow to the subject. It could highlight and illuminate objects in the scene that could be used as leading lines to the subject.

Figure 5.13a Leading lines are an effective way to help focus the viewer's eye. © Disney.

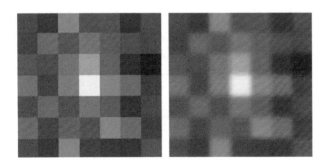

Figure 5.12 Looking at an image through squinted eyes can enable the artist to identify the focal point of the image.

An excellent example is lighters using volumetric lights to lead the viewer's eye. A spotlight is already a cone that normally starts off screen and is focused on the subject matter. If that spotlight's cone becomes visible it can serve as a path to the focal point.

Figure 5.13b Leading lines are an effective way to help focus the viewer's eye.

Figure 5.14 An example of a volumetric light used as leading lines. Still from the animated short *Edmond était un âne* (Edmond was a Donkey). Property of Papy3d/ONF NFB/ARTE.

dark over light   light over dark   contrasting colors

Figure 5.15 Examples of contrasting elements allowing the main subjects to be more prominent. (Left) Still from the animated short *Shave It*. Property of 3DAR. (Center) Still from the animated short *Premier Automne*. Property of *Carlos DeCarvalho*. (Right) Still from the animated short *Mac and Cheese*. Property of Colorbleed Animation Studio.

Figure 5.16 The clutter of leaves creates a pattern that is broken up by the character's face. This interruption in the clutter helps draw the viewer in. Image for *The Secret Life of Kells*. Courtesy of Cartoon Saloon, Les Armateurs and Vivi Film.

Contrasting Elements

In Chapter 1, the concept of creating visual separation between the subject and the background was discussed. The idea was to use either bright elements over dark, dark over light, or complementary colors to get the subject to pop off the background. The core concept is to establish a pattern or anticipated look with one element (color, value, etc.) and then use the contradicting element of that pattern to make the viewer focus on that particular region.

Another example of creating this visual separation can be achieved with shapes. The contrast of cluttered, "busy" shapes with simple, clean shapes can also direct the viewer's eye. By breaking that pattern of visual clutter with a clean center, the audience has the contrasting element to focus on.

Pockets of Light

When lighting, it may be necessary to give the audience multiple focal points. Perhaps the characters are standing on one side of the room and the objects they are searching for are across on the other side. In these particular instances the artist will need to create multiple pockets of light in order for the audience to read all necessary story points. These pockets will guide the audience's eye around the image and allow them to understand the necessary components of the shot.

Another trick is to use pockets of light to construct a visual path for the characters to follow. This works particularly well for traveling sequences or shots when the character's goal is to get from one place to the other. By placing lights to illuminate the intended path, the artist can indicate what the characters are planning and the audience can begin to envision the journey with them.

Figure 5.17 These pockets of light help lead the audience's eye along the pathway the character will follow. Still from the animated short *The Tale of Mr. Revus*, property of Marius Herzog.

Artistically Positioned Shadows

When positioning light to direct the viewer's eye one must focus not only on their illumination but also on the shadows being created. These shadows, if crafted well, can be used to direct the viewer's eye across the screen. Shadows can be used to create swaths of dark sections for a bright object to sit atop. They can visually separate two objects, causing them to appear not only as different pockets of light but also as completely disconnected from one another, as discussed in the "Emphasizing the Mood" section. Elongated shadows also can create a unique line that helps lead the audience's eye to a character that is relatively small on screen, as in Figure 5.18.

Figure 5.18 Artistically positioned shadows can aid the overall composition.

Vignetting

Vignetting is a subtle tool in the never-ending struggle to help the audience center their focus. Vignetting is the darkening around the periphery of the frame allowing the center to obtain more of the attention.

Although it is now used often used as an aesthetic element, vignetting used to be an unintentional and unwanted effect of lens distortion or camera settings. The camera lens creates a circular image on the film plane which is normally cropped, but vignetting occurs when the dark circular shape appears on the frame. An artificial vignette in computer graphics is therefore normally circular or round in shape to mimic this mechanical process.

The aesthetic value of a vignette is the creation of a perimeter or darkened, visual wall around the image. The darker values stop viewers from having a wandering eye that could drift off screen and instead keeps them focused on the brighter subject matter. It can also add an extra element of visual shaping since the vignette gradually darkens over distance and can create a nice falloff toward the side of the frame.

Figure 5.19 This strong vignette pushes the audience's attention to the girl in the center of the screen. Still from the animated short *I, Pet Goat II* and property of Heliofant.

Figure 5.19 Increasing the vignette can help center the focus. Be aware that the stronger the vignette, the more the audience is likely to be aware of it.

Depth of Field

Depth of field is another concept from photography that started as a mechanical flaw of the image-making process but has morphed into a visual aesthetic. Depth of field is the term given to the area of apparent sharpness within the photograph versus the blurred areas in front of or behind the subject.

Three factors, the aperture of the lens, the focal length of the lens, and the distance to the subject, determine depth of field. The aperture is the small opening in a lens that lets the light pass through. The size of that opening will increase the amount of light that enters, but will also influence depth of field. The smaller the aperture, the greater the depth of field. So an aperture setting of f4 will be a much more shallow depth of field than f16. There was even a group of twentieth-century photographers who formed an organization called Group F64 that represented images in sharp

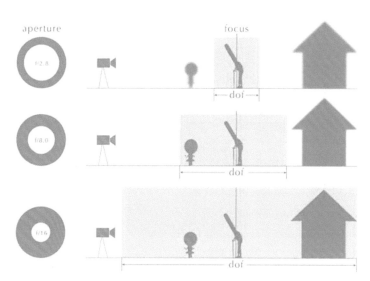

Figure 5.20 The aperture of the lens, the focal length of the lens, and the distance to the subject all play a role in determining depth of field.

Figure 5.21 Adding too much depth of field blur can make large landscape feel microscopic.

Figure 5.22 By shifting the depth of field the artist is also able to shift the viewer's focus.

focus. Group members included famous photographers like Ansel Adams, Imogen Cunningham, and Edward Weston. Thinking of their group name and the images they outputted tends to help artists remember the f-stop/depth of field relationship.

The focal length of the lens also plays a role in depth of field. Wide-angle lenses will increase the depth of field while telephoto lenses decrease it. This is a big factor as to why telephoto images look more compressed than wide-angle ones.

Finally, the distance to camera plays a role in depth of field. The closer the focal point is to the camera, the less depth of field is and the more intense the blur is. Therefore, the same lens with the same aperture will be able to put a larger range in focus when the subject is standing twenty feet away versus one foot away. All these factors must be taken into consideration when determining the amount of depth of field blur to add to a shot.

By blurring elements in the foreground and background the artist can allow only the area around the subject matter to be in focus. This is a great technique, but one that must be done with reference images. If blur is applied too heavily it can make a large scene feel very tiny. Take the photograph in Figure 5.21 as an example. By using a photographic technique called "tilt-shift" the artist is able to take this scene and make it feel like a miniature just by over-emphasizing the depth of field.

This is, of course, a more extreme use of depth of field. Many times when working with animated films, the blurriness will be subtler and less dramatic.

Visual Shaping

Take a moment and stop reading this book. Look around and pick out one object in your current surroundings. Study that object and notice how light is striking it. Even if it is a flat object like a flat wall or hanging picture, there is always some sort of value or hue shift as light make its way across, around, or up the object. Light does not illuminate an object uniformly. In 3D, it is these value differences that an artist simulates in order to create good visual shaping.

If anyone has ever looked at a CG image and thought it looked fake, it is almost certainly because it lacked visual shaping. Even a pure white wall will still have variation to it. The wall will be slightly brighter as it gets closer to a window or other light source in the room. If there is an overhead light, the value will shift darker as it vertically descends the wall.

If there is a lamp on an end table, notice the shape of the light on the wall directly surrounding that light source.

Even if the lighting is purely even, a child's handprint, some markings from furniture, or a slight warping of the wall will stop it from being evenly illuminated all the time. The world is full of such complex and subtle details that, when overly flat objects appear lacking in shape, the audience will know there is something false about it. The world is

Figure 5.23 Creating visual shaping and variation across all surfaces, even flat ones, is essential to successful visual shaping.

an extremely messy place and anything that looks too perfect just reads as fake.

Take this example from the Dutch Golden Age painter Willem Claeszoon Heda (Figure 5.24). Notice the variation within each object. At no point in the painting does the value of the color remain the same for very long. The bread roll at the front of the table, the specular variation in the glass and metal objects, the reflections in the plate, the way the white tablecloth lightens and darkens at every crease, everything has variation. Even the wall behind the scene has light variation that provides shaping and directs the viewer's eye to the still life. It is this type of subtle shaping that allows a man-made image to look organic and believable.

Figure 5.24 *Still Life with Oysters, a Rummer, a Lemon and a Silver Bowl* (1634), oil on canvas, Rijksmuseum, Amsterdam. **This painting by Willem Claeszoon Heda demonstrates exceptional shaping across all the objects in the scene.**

Painting with Light

Often people equate a CG lighter to a photographer positioning lights around a studio. In the natural world, photographers and filmmakers are confined to working with existing natural light and are only able to add additional light through using artificial light sources, bounce cards, or other practical lighting techniques. Rarely do they start with the absence of any light, as a CG lighter would. Even in that situation a photographer is still handcuffed by the physics of light in his or her work.

CG lighters, like painters, are not confined by those restrictions. They can push, pull, twist, and bend light in whatever way they wish to achieve the desired look. While an understanding of the physics of light is absolutely crucial, the lighting artist does not want to break the audience's level of believability. A lighter has free rein to use any means necessary to make the simulated world more beautiful. In the CG world, unlike photography, there are no laws of physics or pre-existing natural light that must be harnessed in order to achieve the shot. Like painting, the CG world starts off as a blank canvas. All light must be created, warped, and positioned in just the way the artist wants.

One of the most concrete examples of visual shaping was developed during the Dutch Renaissance when painters utilized a lighting technique now known as Rembrandt Lighting. Rembrandt Lighting is best identified by one main key light positioned on one side of the character. The light is roughly positioned 45 degrees to the side and 45 degrees above the character, creating subtle falloff from the main key side across to the opposite side of the face emphasizing the volume of the character. One of the biggest indicators that Rembrandt Lighting is being used is the telltale "triangle of light" that forms on the fill side of the character's cheek as light sneaks past the bridge of the nose..

The term "Rembrandt Lighting" has been credited to Cecil B. DeMille when he was describing his innovative use of artificial lighting in the early days of modern cinema.

DeMille and his set and lighting designer, Wilfred Buckland, had both been trained by Broadway producer, David Belasco, known for his brilliant lighting techniques. DeMille explained in his autobiography that while shooting *The Warrens of Virginia* (1915), he borrowed some portable spotlights from the Mason Opera House in downtown Los Angeles and "began to make shadows where shadows would appear in nature."

When business partner Sam Goldwyn saw the film with only half an actor's face illuminated, he feared the exhibitors would pay only half the price for the picture. After DeMille told him it was Rembrandt lighting, "Sam's reply was jubilant with relief: for Rembrandt lighting the exhibitors would pay double!"

http://www.cecilbdemille.com/legacy.html

triangle of light

Figure 5.25 Notice the triangle of light beneath Rembrandt's eye in this self-portrait. Rembrandt Harmenszoon van Rijn, *Rembrandt autoportrait aux mains sur les hanches* (Self-portrait with the hands on the hips) (1632).

Figure 5.26a This Rembrandt Lighting triangle can also be achieved by positioning the key light in the CG scene.

Examples of Rembrandt Lighting can be found in a wide variety of films, television shows, and animated work. It is successful because it creates a good volumetric representation of the shape of the face. The lighting is dramatic yet soft enough to flatter the subject being lit. All the contours and attributes are brought to life and the viewer gets a good sense of space and depth in this otherwise two-dimensional medium.

Figure 5.26b Image courtesy of Rocky McCorkle and from the series *You and Me on a Sunny Day.*

The Ansel Adams Zone System

Rembrandt Lighting is an excellent technique in helping to teach artists how to position a key light to create good visual shaping on a character. An example of creating successful value variation is the Ansel Adams zone system. Adams and fellow photographer Fred Archer created the zone system back in the 1930s as a guide to creating a variety of tones in a photographic image.

The zone system's goal is to create proper exposures at the time of shooting a photograph to achieve an appropriate range of zones. This system categorizes the values of an image into eleven groups ranging from black to white. In photography, each zone represents an f-stop of exposure, but for the final image it breaks the image down into components and tonal ranges in the chart in Figure 5.27a.

It is not completely necessary for all zones to be hit for an image to be successful. This just exemplifies one technique for creating a range of values in a shot. In these examples, it is apparent how almost every zone is represented in each image and how that can translate to an overall visually stimulating product.

The artist may ask how this relates to images being created with computer graphics. One would assume that computer animation generally works in color and this black to white range only applies to black and white images. The truth is that one trick artists use when analyzing their work is to strip the color out and make the image black and white in order to analyze the tonal range. This can be achieved by desaturating the image in an image editing tool. The artist can then analyze the luminosity of the image without color to help gain an understanding of whether the overall tonal

Figure 5.27a The Ansel Adams zone system categorizes values into numeric values ranging from 0 to 10.

range of the image is working. Often with color images it is easy to get lost in their hues and tones and lose focus of just the simple grayscale image to ensure that there is variation in the luminance and that the brightest point is where the audience should be looking. This grayscale version will allow the artist to just see masses and get a better understanding of the overall tonal balance of the shot. If the black to white version of the shot is weak and flat, the image will suffer as a result.

Figure 5.27b Examples of photographs that demonstrate a full range of values across the image.

Figure 5.27c Achieving this full range of values is just as important in a CG image as it is in photography. Still from the animated short *The Fantastic Flying Books of Mr. Morris Lessmore*. Property of Moonbot Studios.

Final Thoughts

Once these basic elements of a well-lit shot are identified, it is difficult to look at an image the same way. The artist can begin to dissect shots in such a way that will allow individual elements to emerge. What is the mood being created by these colors and light qualities? How does this image create shaping? Where is my eye being drawn and why? This understanding and analysis will not only improve the artist's eye when viewing the work of others, but also when analyzing one's own images and looking for ways to improve them.

Interview
with Josh Staub

Visual Effects Supervisor :: Walt Disney Animation Studios.

Q. What is your current job/role at your company?
A. I've been at Walt Disney Animation Studios for eight years, most recently serving as Visual Effects Supervisor on the short film *Feast*, but prior to that I was a Lighting Supervisor on the animated feature films *Frozen* and *Tangled*. My first film at Disney was as a Lighting and Compositing Artist on *Bolt*.

Q. What inspired you to become an artist on CG films?
A. Prior to coming to Disney I spent almost fourteen years at a game company called Cyan Worlds (most known for the games *Myst and Riven*). At Cyan I wore many hats—Artist, Production Designer, Art Director, Game Designer—but after several years there I began to feel pulled towards the film industry, specifically because of the linear storytelling aspect. It had gotten frustrating for me to work in games where, from the "storyteller's" perspective, you give up control to the audience (the player) to determine how your work is experienced. This was also at a time when CG animated fFilms, most notably those by Pixar—*Finding Nemo, The Incredibles, Ratatouille*—were really pushing the genre forward in terms of visual storytelling.

Q. What non-CG artwork inspires you?
A. Wow, where to begin! I'm inspired by traditional art forms—painting, drawing, and photography in particular. I tend to be pretty polished with my own drawings and paintings, so artists like José Manuel Fernández Oli, Yannick Dusseault, Kazuo Oga (known for his incredible Studio Ghibli background paintings), and Craig Mullins are right up my alley. They have an incredible understanding of light so

even when they paint stylistically there is a natural quality to their work that I find appealing. On the other end of the spectrum (I suppose because opposites attract), I'm mesmerized by the design qualities of Kevin Dart, Tadahiro Uesugi, and Charley Harper. Ironically, a lot of the incredible artists I just mentioned often work digitally, but with today's tools being what they are the lines are so blurred I don't make much of a distinction any more.

Q. What are your key components to a well-lit shot? In other words, what are the handful of requirements every shot must have in order to be successful?

A. First and foremost, shots should be clearly and easily readable. The viewer's eye should quickly focus on the important part of the image. They should also be appealing—this is particularly important when it comes to characters. Characters designed to be beautiful should look beautiful under any lighting condition. Furthermore, successfully lit shots are believable, balanced, and maintain continuity with the shots around them when applicable. Finally, the most effective shots are lit in a way that enhances the story by using mood and drama to evoke the proper emotional response from the audience.

Q. Color obviously plays a large role in lighting. Can you discuss some of the ways that you use color to help set the mood of your lighting designs?

A. Color has an obvious role in setting a particular mood—cooler colors evoke a sense of calm and quietness, warm colors are vibrant and energetic, red being the most exciting. In general terms I tend to use colors that create a contrast between light and shadow—for example, I often balance warm key lighting with cooler shadows, and cool key lighting will play off warmer shadows. Keeping the shadows saturated is important—particularly when lighting characters—as shadows can tend to look grey, yielding an unappealing ghostly or cadaverous appearance. Management of colors within the image is also important. Bright colors away from the point of focus can be distracting to the eye, so I will often mute them (artificially in the composite if necessary).

Q. Do you have any specific tricks or techniques you use for generating good visual shaping?

A. No particular tricks or techniques aside from trying to keep the lighting setup as simple as possible. Too many lights results in complex light shapes and shadows which yield an unappealing image. I spend most of my time simply on the basic fill light and the direction of the key light and its resulting shadow shape. Once I'm happy with that I move on to whatever bounces I need, followed by a rim when necessary to serve as icing on the cake to help the character (or object of focus) pop. I tend to try and get a lit image into the composite as soon as possible and work back and forth between the lighting and compositing stage. Having said that, I try and do as much as possible in the lighting and almost nothing in the comp except for enhancements (subtle blooms, depth of field modifications, slight color tweaks, etc.) because I believe it results in the simplest setup and yields the clearest and most impactful image.

Q. Are there certain ways you like to draw the viewer's eye to a certain section of the image?
A. There are many ways to draw the viewer's eye, but I tend to think of it in terms of value structure first. Putting the object of interest in a pool of light surrounded by dimmer and less interesting lighting is generally effective. Areas of high contrast draw the eye as well so using a strong rim or putting the object of interest in silhouette surrounded by bright lighting also works. Color is obviously another way of achieving this: bright colors will draw the eye—a strong warm color surrounded by a sea of cool, for example. Last but not least, depth of field is another great tool which helps let the viewer know subconsciously where they should be looking. Of course, these techniques should be chosen only to serve the purpose of communicating the story and mood—the misuse of these techniques can have devastating consequences and leave the audience confused. For example, pushing the amount of depth of field too far can make a scene feel miniature, a character placed in silhouette will evoke drama that may be unintended, etc.

Q. When looking at a demo reel, what are the elements you look for to show the applicant has the ability to create a well-lit shot?
A. Number one, only put your best work on the reel. It should really be about quality, and not quantity. Having said that, there should be enough variety to show that you are capable of executing a number of different styles. For example, having a shot or two of both photorealistic and stylized work is helpful. Furthermore, still images are nice, but it's much more difficult to execute a shot with an animated character which is most of what you will be doing should you land your dream job anyway, so make sure most (if not all) of your shots include motion. As I mentioned earlier, every shot should be clear and easy to read—when looking at a reel I should know exactly where I'm supposed to look the moment the image appears on screen.

Q. Where do you think the future of lighting is headed?
A. I believe we are at a very important moment in the industry in terms of lighting. We now have the ability to create images that are completely natural and photorealistic, and there are times when photorealism can and should be the goal. However, just because we can create an image that looks photorealistic doesn't mean we should! There is no limit now to what we are technically and artistically capable of achieving visually, so—and this sounds incredibly cheesy I know—the only limit is our imagination. Let's see how far we can push it in as many unique directions as possible.

Q. If you could tell yourself one piece of advice when you were first starting out in this industry, what would it be?
A. The greatest piece of advice I would give to myself just starting out would be to keep the story in the forefront of my mind with every shot, make sure that every decision I make enhances the story visually by providing clarity and purpose. The end result should be beautiful, but if my choices confuse or distract from the story the lighting has failed to do its job. The other piece of advice I would give myself is to never stop learning—be a great listener and be humble and open to any and all input and direction.

Q. In your opinion, what makes a good lighting artist?
A. First and foremost, a great lighter has a fantastic eye and is a wonderful visual storyteller. They are masters of versatility. They are able to work both alone and in teams and take artistic direction well, while also thoughtfully promoting their own ideas. Technically, they must be capable of managing high levels of complexity while maintaining an organized workflow. They are able to produce inspiring work even under intense time constraints and pressure, while keeping a positive attitude.

6

Lighting Scenarios

Lighting has some basic general characteristics that are applicable to any scene. Creating mood, directing the viewer's eye, and creating visual shaping are all valid regardless of the specific situation. There are, however, specific components to different lighting scenarios that demand special requirements and needs. What characteristics make up successful beauty lighting for a character? How does one approach lighting a character's eye? What are some of the tricks for lighting an interior environment versus an exterior? These are the types of questions this chapter will explore.

Still from the animated short *Shave It*. Property of 3DAR.

Character Lighting

In most animated films, the character is the driving element for the story. Characters act out a performance and the audience normally focuses on these characters for the majority of the film. Because of this focused attention, developing and pushing character lighting is crucial to a visually successful animated project. In previous chapters this book discussed the use of Rembrandt Lighting in characters as a means of generating shaping, but there is more that can be done to make the characters shine.

Hero Color

Characters in animated films generally have an ideal color. *Shrek* has a specific green. Woody has his warm hue. The Minions of *Despicable Me* have a very distinct yellow color. This color is often described as being the "hero color" for that character. The lighting artist must make sure the character's hero color is present and identifiable regardless of the lighting scenario. This is achieved by crafting lights with specific hues and intensities to make the hero color apparent.

This becomes especially important when the overall color design of a scene is a complementary color to the hero color of the character. Say there is a cool-toned character with blue fur. If that character were placed next to warm candlelight, the artist would take special attention to ensure the character's cool tones are not being too contaminated with the warm light. These conflicting values can not only take the character away from the hero hue, but

Figure 6.1 The lighting on the left allows the true hero color of the character to stand out while the cooler lighting on the right works against his warm hues and actually makes him look discolored and sickly. Pio is downloadable character courtesy of Boutique23 (www.boutique23.com).

also desaturate and gray the character, often making them look ill.

Take Miranda from this sequence in Brave (Figure 6.2). Her main iconic element is her fiery red hair. If the artist had chosen to have the cool surroundings influence it too much, then the warmth of the hair would be desaturated and weak. Her skin tone would also suffer by looking washed out and sickly. These warm tones also aid in readability since her skin and hair help her stand out from not only the cool colored surroundings, but also the glowing orb which is the object of her gaze.

Of course, this doesn't mean that the artist completely ignores the lighting scenario. If no care is given to the surroundings, the character will look out of place or as if the character does not belong in that environment. Instead the artist must find the balance between integrating the characters into the scene and making the character match the hero color. This can be a difficult challenge, but by identifying and using good reference it can be achieved.

Figure 6.2 Miranda's red hair is kept recognizable and iconic in all lighting situations. © Disney.

Figure 6.3 Techniques of getting a character to read include light over dark (top right), saturation over desaturated (top left), warm over cool (bottom left), and sometimes dark over light (bottom right). Still from the animated short *Shave It* (bottom left). Property of 3DAR. Still from the animated short *The Missing Scarf* (top left). Property of Eoin Duffy. Still from the animated short *Juste de l'eau* (top right). Property of Carlos DeCarvalho. Still from the animated short *The Fantastic Flying Books of Mr. Morris Lessmore* (bottom right). Property of Moonbot Studios.

More Defined Focus

Character lighting often involves getting the audience to focus on the area of the character most significant to the story. Often characters are talking and exchanging dialog so the focus should be on the face, specifically the eyes. Other times characters are pointing at something or holding an important object and the artist needs the audience to focus on the hands. There could also be a situation where the character is standing in a significant spot so the artist needs to focus the gaze down toward the feet. In each of these cases it is the lighter's job to nudge the viewer's eye in the right direction.

The best way to accomplish this is to over-emphasize whatever technique is being used to get the character to stand out from the background in the first place. If the character is light and the background is dark, then the area of focus will become slightly brighter.

If the character is dark over a light background, perhaps the area just around the head is slightly brighter in the background. If it is a difference of saturation, like cool character over a warmer background, one option could be to make the focal point a touch more saturated and slightly brighter in value. These increases should be minor and almost unperceivable by the audience. The shift between the light and dark sections should be a nice, smooth transition that never pushes the values into blown-out whites or deep blacks.

Specularity for Variation

It is a constant battle for lighting artists to continuously create shaping in characters. One of the tools for this is specularity. Whether they are covered in skin, fur, feathers, or scales, characters can often have significant specular values that can be controlled to create shaping. Beginning artists will see a section of a character that is looking flat and uninteresting and immediately push diffuse light to that region to create variation. This can lead to characters looking overly lit and not properly falling off in the shadowed areas. Often, especially in fill/bounce areas, adding a light that emits specularity only will create the right amount of variation without adding diffuse light. This is especially true with long hair as the specularity will show off some sheen and shape.

Figure 6.4 By adding specular values across the back of the head of this robot the artist was able to avoid flat shapes and generate successful shaping. Still from the animated short *L3.0*. Property of Pierre Jury, Vincent Defour, Cyril Declercq, Alexis Decelle, and ISART DIGITAL (school).

Framing the Character

Using light and structural elements in a scene to frame a character is important to help focus attention. Staging the scene so that surrounding elements visually encompass the character is extremely important. Additionally, a lighter can light these elements in such a way for the framing to be more successful. The lighter can rim these elements to get their shapes to read. Another way is to construct dark values around the focal point to help frame the action. Additionally, the artist must actively avoid visual intersections or tangents between a character and the background. This does not mean the character is actually intersecting with other geometry.

What it means is that background elements are awkwardly placed to slash through or stick out of the character in 2D space. For example, the branch of a tree coming into a frame and visually sticking into the side of the head of the character would exemplify this concept. From a lighting standpoint, this could be a hard shadow that goes right through the middle of the character, visually cutting him in half. By moving this distracting background shadow the artist can create a stronger composition.

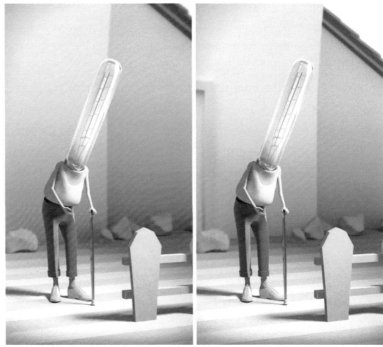

Figure 6.5 The lamp post and carriage do an excellent job framing the action in this shot. Still from the animated short *The Picture of Dorian Grey.* Property of Tom Beg.

Figure 6.6 In this example, the corner of the wall is bisecting the character's head and is distracting. By repositioning the camera slightly the artist is able to create a better composition.

Eyes

It is impossible to discuss character lighting without mentioning the eyes. Creating well-lit eyes is absolutely necessary for building a connection between the audience and the character. The eyes are what give a character a soul and can make the audience feel there is more than what exists on the surface. If ever an audience describes a CG character as looking "dead" or "unnatural" it is almost always because the eyes are not right. The specific description can even be termed as "dead-eyed." Animators can create beautiful, subtle emotion in the eyes, but if the lighter does not make those movements come to life it is all for naught.

Anatomy of the Eye

In order to understand how an eye should be lit the artist should have a general understanding of the anatomy of an eye. Other animals have different eye geometry from human beings, but the human-like eye is given to almost all CG characters since audiences are more comfortable connecting with that look. The human eye is made up of two main sections that should be replicated in the geometry. The first is the outer, clear layer that protects the eye, known as the cornea. This is the clear lens that is wet and gives the eye its visually reflective quality. The inner part of the eye is made up of a sphere with one concave dimple that is the central, functioning area of the eye. This inner sphere is broken up into three parts: the sclera (the white part of the eye), the iris (the "colored" part of the eye), and the pupil (the black circle at the center of the eye).

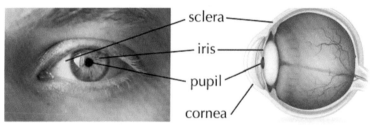

Figure 6.7 The top image demonstrates how different a crocodile's eye is from a human's. The bottom image diagrams the major anatomy points that need to be understood when lighting a human eye.

It is important that the eye geometry in the 3D scene be modeled to mimic this setup. Eyes have a unique way of interacting with light and will only look natural to the audience if created a certain way. If the eye were simply just one sphere, the artist would not be able to achieve the same depth and accuracy necessary for the audience to connect with the character. The audience may not

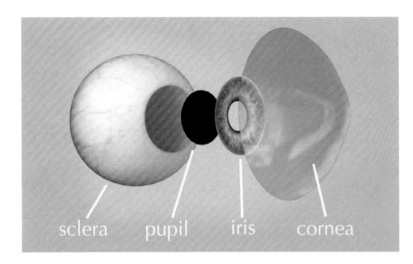

Figure 6.8 The eye geometry should consist of a spherical sclera, a concave iris, and a pupil, all inside a clear cornea.

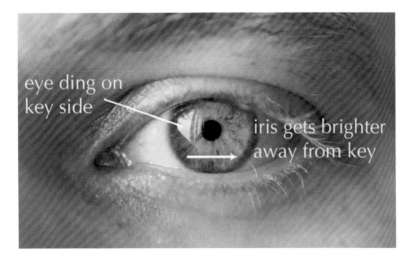

Figure 6.9 The iris is illuminated on the side opposite of the key due to its concave shape.

be able to identify exactly what those characteristics are, but they will know when they are not present.

The first element necessary for successful eye lighting is creating good overall shaping. The sclera works pretty much like any other sphere. The light should be brighter on the key side and get darker toward the fill. The iris is where it becomes interesting. Since the iris is on a concave slope, the key side of the iris is actually angled away from the light while the opposite side is facing the key. Therefore, it is the opposite side of the iris that gets the illumination while the key side is darker.

Generally speaking, the artist wants the eye whites to be the brightest part on the face. This makes sense since they are mostly white and the artist wants the audience to connect to the character by looking him or her in the eye. The difficulty arises when they need to be bright while still maintaining shaping and, most importantly, not "blowing out" or becoming too overly lit. The overall value of the eye white is very sensitive and must be treated delicately.

The sclera, iris, and pupil must all be visible as three separate sections. This can often be a problem between the iris and the pupil. If the iris becomes too dark and blends with the pupil, the result will appear as though the character has either black eyes or one large pupil. The iris must also not become too intense in value or saturation. This will make the character look bizarre and potentially insane. Striking that proper balance is key.

All of these specifications can lead to eyes being lit separately from the rest of the character or independently adjusted in the composite. This is fine but the artist must remember that while the eye is the brightest part of the face, it must not stand out too much and must feel integrated with the lighting of the rest of the face. This is especially true at the point where the eyeball meets the eyelid. There should be some darkening or occlusion taking place that allows the eye to sit back into place behind the eyelids.

As mentioned previously, there is a cornea that sits on top of the sclera, iris, and pupil. This is a thin, wet, transparent membrane that protects the front of the eye. Visually, the cornea provides two main looks. The first is the reflective quality of the eye. The cornea will not only reflect the area immediately surrounding the eye, like eyelashes or glasses, but also the scene surrounding the character. Therefore, it may be important to create a reflection pass for just the cornea on close-up shots to show what the character is looking at.

The other main visual contribution of the cornea is the eye ding. The eye ding is the specular highlight in the eye that is normally the reflection of the key light. Eye dings give the character's eyes more depth and personality. They can either be a circular dot created by a spotlight emitting specular only and linked to the cornea or, for a more realistic look, they could mimic the actual shape of an object or key light in the scene through the eye reflection. The artist generally only wants one ding light per eye. The ding will be brighter on the key side and slightly dimmer on the fill side. It should be on the key side of the eye and mimic the color of the key light. The ding is best when positioned on the border between either the iris and pupil or iris and sclera. It usually works best when at the ten o'clock or two o'clock position on the eye and it should never fall into the center of the eye.

When the eye is animated, this can get tricky. Often artists initially want to parent the eye ding/spec light to the eye position, but that is a bad idea. Remember, the eye ding is meant to mimic the key light, so if the key light is stationary, the ding should be stationary too. That isn't to say the artist should not animate the position of the eye ding slightly to keep it aesthetically pleasing, but the audience should not perceive movement. With the proper technique and finesse this animation could be subtle and unseen. Better yet, the artist can hide the animated movement of the eye ding in the character's blinks. So everything is stationary until the two or three frames as the character blinks and then the artist can shift things around as the dings are hidden.

Eye Lighting Checklist

- Sclera is shaped well toward the key side
- Iris is shaped well opposite the key side
- All three areas of the eye are distinguishable
- The sclera is the brightest part of the face without blowing out
- There is one eye ding
- It is at the 10:00 or 2:00 position and generally stays in that spot
- The eye ding mimics the color and shape of the key

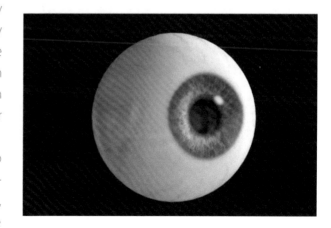

Figure 6.10 A checklist for creating successful eye lighting.

Interior Lighting

Lighting interior spaces could be one of the trickiest tasks for a lighter. How does exterior light enter the space and influence the look? What if there are light sources inside the space? What color are those lights and how do they illuminate the room? There are a number of extremely subtle elements that must be balanced with great care in order to get the final look to be successful.

Various Light Colors and Intensities

Interior lighting contains a wide array of different light sources. There can be direct sunlight, window light, tungsten lamps, fluorescent lamps, candlelight, and countless others. Each one of these light sources varies in intensity and contains a great range of colors. Tungsten light bulbs and candles normally look orange/yellow and can create a nice warm tone to a space. Fluorescent lights are much cooler and can even have a green cast. Natural light coming in through the windows will have a wide variety of colors depending on time of day.

When balancing light intensities between interior sources and exterior sources, it is important to remember that the human eye has the dynamic range to allow humans to see what is outside and inside the space at the same time. Photographic images do not work the same way. Almost always, the artist would need to decide whether to expose the film so the exterior is balanced properly but the interior is very dark. Or the interior light is exposed correctly and the exterior light is glowing white and the landscape is difficult to perceive. So in trying to replicate a photorealistic environment the artist must respect this limitation of photography and create an image that replicates that look.

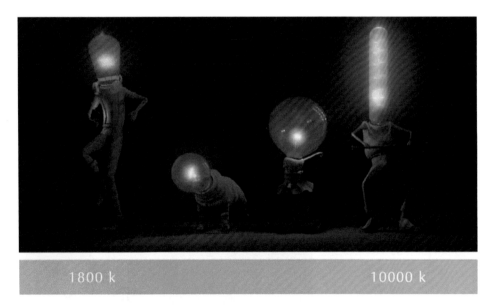

1800 k   10000 k

Figure 6.11 Light color can widely vary from cool to warm depending on the specific light source.

Figure 6.12 It is rare to have exposure levels the same inside a building as outside. The artist usually must choose either to make the outside extremely bright and the inside properly balanced or to have the inside go dark as the outside has the proper exposure.

Artificial Interior Light Sources

One of the main light sources when dealing with interior spaces in modern times is the lamp. Lamps come in many varieties and each has its own specific qualities. The bulbs themselves can have unique shapes and can cast many different colors depending on whether they are tungsten, LED, or CFLs. These lights can be simulated in CG using different methods depending on the renderer, but the key is

Figure 6.13 When analyzing interior lights, it is important to pay attention to the color, intensity, and how far the light travels into the room.

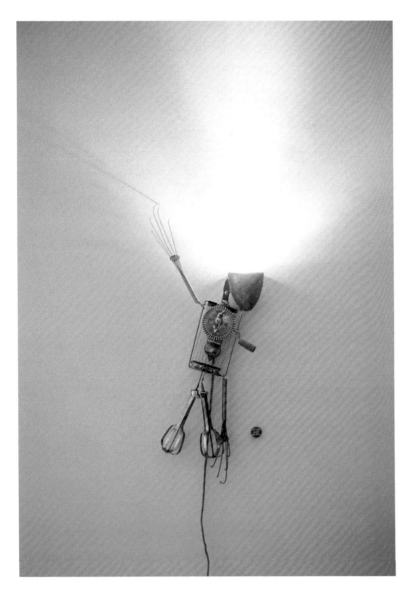

Figure 6.14 It is important to evaluate the shape the light makes on the wall as well.

to identify the main attributes of the light being simulated with reference and artistically recreate it.

There are a few key elements that should be identified when trying to replicate any artificial light source. The first is light color and intensity, mentioned in the previous section. How bright is the spot on the wall closest to the light source? How far does that particular light's influence reach? How much light shines through the shade? How much does that shade influence the color of the light hitting the wall?

The second is the shape created when that particular light source interacts with the surrounding environment. Some lamps use traditional bulbs that allow the light to directly hit the wall, while some lamps have an element the light passes through before reaching the surroundings. Other lamps are similar to car headlights in that the bulb is pointed at a reflective surface and bounces the light into the world. This often causes a pattern or shape to form on surrounding surfaces. Additionally, depending on the age and state of the light, this reflective element could be disfigured and shine asymmetrically.

While there are countless nuances that could be factored into the final look, another major element that must always be considered is the shape of the cast shadow of the lamp or shade onto the surroundings. Depending on the size of the bulb, the distance between the bulb and the object being lit, the distance between the light source and the wall, and the type of lampshade, this shadow shape can change dramatically.

Window Lighting

One of the most intriguing elements of interior lighting is dealing with the combination of interior artificial lights with exterior natural light. The natural light often comes streaming in through windows and has a certain aesthetic quality. This look is extremely common to those in the modern world and should be replicated accurately in order to ensure the believability.

Moonlight and sunlight shining through windows have visually parallel light rays. This means the shadow created by the window onto the floor is parallel and does not warp in any way. The way the shadow looks at the bottom of the window is the same as the look of the shadow at the top. They are not elongated or foreshortened because that gives the wrong visual indicator. This will make the light source feel too unnaturally close to the window and it will no longer feel like sunlight or moonlight.

Light rays get diffused when passing through glass and this causes the light and shadow quality to get a bit softer. The level of this diffusion depends on the specific type of glass but the shadows cast inside a building are always a little softer than if the scene were outside because of this window diffusion. One thing to remember with daytime window light is that it is not only the sunlight that is shining through. The artist must account for the color of the sky and any other exterior elements that would penetrate through the window.

Figure 6.15 It is always interesting working with the color combination of warm tungsten light with the much cooler daylight.

Figure 6.16 Examples of a "cooler" and "warmer" white balance.

White Balance

Whether a photographer, a painter, or a lighter, all artists must consider how to handle balancing the color of various light sources of an interior scene. "White balance" is a term used in photography and filmmaking. It refers to balancing the color to determine the white point of an image. Therefore, white balance settings can be used to balance out either the warm hues of daylight or the cool hues of nighttime. The difficulty is what to do when you have both warm and cool light in a scene.

Consider an example. There may be cool moonlight shining through the window and warm lamps on the interior. Does the artist balance the color to neutralize the cool exterior but increase the warm look of the interior? Or does the artist balance the white level to the interior allowing the cool tones coming through the window to be saturated? In CG lighting, the artist has the ability to control these values. Figuring out the proper balance between the various type of light sources will go a long way in determining the final look of the shot.

Walls and Corners

Interior light does not illuminate a flat wall evenly. The closer a section of a wall is to the light source, the brighter that section will be. The more exposed the walls are, the more ambient light they will receive. Therefore, the wide part of the wall will be brighter than the corners since it is more exposed to ambient light. This shift as the eye travels down the wall is subtle, but crucial when striving to replicate accurate interior light.

The connection points between walls, ceilings, and floors are also crucial areas. Many times inexperienced artists will create very hard lines between these elements. This is normally a result of light linking causing certain lights to hit one wall but not the ceiling they are connected to. This results in a visual problem where there is a drastic light and color difference between the two surfaces that are merely inches apart. It is therefore important to always ensure that the walls, ceilings and floors are always well balanced and create a seamless flow throughout the space as they would in the real world.

Subtle Shaping and Bounce

Many interior lighting scenarios come down to one major question: Can the artist create visual interest and subtle shaping around a space dominated by a variety of light sources and a lot of bounce and fill lights? This is no easy feat for anyone to accomplish, let alone new artists. Much practice and repetition are necessary before successful, consistent interior images can be completed. Always remember to have a good reference to keep on track and focused.

Figure 6.17 Notice the varying values as the light moves up and down the wall.

Exterior Lighting

Landscapes present an array of challenges to the lighting artist that mostly center on the perception of scale. Not always will the set contain humans or common objects that will give the audience a size reference to work with. Sometimes it is the lighter's job to communicate that scale successfully through subtle hints and replicating natural phenomena.

It is of the utmost importance for lighting artists to understand aerial perspective. Aerial perspective, or atmospheric perspective, is

Figure 6.18 Still from the animated short *Mac and Cheese*. Property of Colorbleed Animation Studio.

Figure 6.19 Notice how the mountains appear cooler and have less contrast as they fall back into space.

Figure 6.20 Extremely abstract backgrounds can be used to keep the audience focused on the foreground elements. © Disney.

the perception of objects changing appearance as they fall back into space. They lose detail around the edges and, internally, become less saturated and lose contrast as they recede from the camera. Aerial perspective is something that has been analyzed and duplicated in painting for hundreds of years. Although the practice of creating aerial perspective was long established, Leonardo da Vinci was the first to use the term and wrote about it in *Treatise on Painting*: "Colors become weaker in proportion to their distance from the person who is looking at them."

This atmospheric presence is caused by moisture and particles in the air scattering light as it passes. Depending on the wavelength of the light, the scattering of light will vary. Blue light fades away the slowest and, therefore, objects will generally shift toward cooler tones as they fall back into space.

In nature, elevation also plays a large role in determining aerial perspective. The base of a mountain will have more aerial perspective than the peak since the density of the atmosphere is greater at lower elevations. There are also pockets of atmosphere that form in crevices around the mountain that can also lead to varying scatter amounts. The importance in images that lean towards the more photoreal is to include subtle variation within the look of the aerial perspective.

All that being said, animated films will artistically craft aerial perspective to adapt it to a certain aesthetic. This was especially true of the early Disney features like *Bambi* that would often use very beautiful, colorful, abstract backgrounds with dense atmospherics to keep the attention on the characters.

Gobos

Gobo lights play a large role in lighting exteriors. Frequently there are wide swaths of land in a CG scene that can appear very even and boring. Using gobo lighting to simulate clouds in the sky and to break up the illumination of a vast landscape is a common practice. This will not only allow for some visual shaping and variation, it will also provide scale to the scene. The more light variation on a particular object, the larger it normally appears.

Figure 6.21 The shadows from the clouds break up the landscape and help give the terrain a sense of scale. In computer graphics this would best be achieved with a gobo.

God Rays

God rays are a specific type of volumetric light that can occur in nature when the lighting conditions are suitable. This will happen when the sun breaks through the clouds and a radial light ray is formed. This can be incredibly beautiful in nature and can also be commonly used in animated projects to make an environment seem friendlier or more romantic. Ultimately, god rays are an extremely beautiful natural occurrence that a lighting artist has at his or her disposal to deploy when necessary.

Figure 6.22 Notice how the god rays can emanate out from the sun in a radial pattern.

Balancing Black Points

This is similar to aerial perspective but the artist must take special consideration regarding the black points on an environment. Black points refer to the spot that is the absolute darkest. That darkest area is referred to as the black point of that image or region of the image.

The simple concept to remember is that the black point is darkest close to the camera and gets slightly lifted as you move back into space. Black points in distant background objects that are too black can jump off an image and right into the face of the viewer. This will break the illusion of depth and space and can be problematic. The key is to always keep the blackest blacks closer to camera and let the values become slightly lifted as they fall back into space.

Figure 6.23 As the image recesses back into space, the black point is raised and the difference can be quite dramatic.

Final Thoughts

It must always be remembered that tips like the ones given in this chapter are just general guidelines and not hardened rules. Lighting is a fluid process and the artist must always be ready to adjust in order to make a successful image. These are simply tips learned over years of experience and ones that are generally considered good practice. The key is to establish the goal look with reference, identify the key elements of that look, then do whatever it takes to hit those key elements and make the shot look great!

Interview
with Haji Uesato

Lighting Supervisor :: Blue Sky Studios.

Q. How long have you been at your current company?
A. I've been a Lighter at Blue Sky Studios since 2000. I was the Lighting Supervisor of *Epic* and *Ice Age: Dawn of the Dinosaurs*.

Q. Do you have a favorite light?
A. No, but I do have a least favorite light—the key.

Q. What's your beef with the key light?
A. Don't get suckered in by the key, it's overrated. The easiest way to ruin a shot is to become overly dependent on the contribution of the key light. If you're not careful, it can really get away from you. You know, like that loudmouth at a party who shouts over everyone and keeps calling attention to himself inappropriately. Understanding the ambient conditions of your scene needs to come first. When I start a shot, I ignore the key. I'll light it as if a cloud has passed in front of the sun or as if bulbs have burnt out. The scene you light isn't dark or flat, it's subtly shaped by ambient sources. All the objects and characters must be given body and weight. Once the scene looks believable like that—balanced without any overriding directionality—then adding in the key will only make things better. Starting with a key light and filling in around it can get you into trouble fast. It might look okay at first but once you start moving lights around to hit notes, the holes will reveal themselves.

Q. What is the role of the key, then?

A. Every shot in a film is designed with a purpose. As a lighter, your first responsibility is to understand that purpose and what your shot must contribute to progress the story. Mood is established in large part by ambient lighting. You introduce the key light to upset the equilibrium of the ambient environment and use its color and directionality judiciously to tip the overall composition in a way that reinforces the narrative trajectory of the shot.

Q. What makes for great shot lighting?

A. Lighting is fundamentally about composition. This book covers the artistic and technical concepts necessary to direct the viewer's eye. Shots in a feature film are on screen for only a few seconds so a well-lit shot must quickly establish hierarchy in the frame and focus the audience's attention on what's important to the story.

Q. So the key to good lighting is story?

A. A shot will look good if it's doing the right thing. Unlike in live action, in CG production the saying would go "Camera, Action, Lights!" CG lighters have the benefit of beginning their work with the contributions of the other disciplines already in place. In every shot you light, all the artists in the pipeline before you have used the tools of their trades to reinforce a story point. It's all there for you already, you just need to understand it and then use the compositional tools of lighting to shape the image so that the audience will, too.

7

Materials and Compositing

Being a lighting artist or lighting TD can involve a wide range of responsibilities depending on the studio or company. Being a lighter could mean not only creating and positioning lights, but also handling all the materials and shaders for the scene as well. Some studios have a separate shading department that creates all the material and texture files. The same is true with regard to compositing. In other studios, lighters assemble all their render layers into a final composite and are responsible for outputting the final image that will appear on screen. There are also pipelines in which the lighters pass shots off to compositors or stereoscopic artists to bring the shot across the finish line. In the end, each studio and project functions a little differently.

Either way, it is essential for lighters to have a good understanding of how materials and compositing play a role in the overall look in order to complete the job successfully. Because, at the end of the day, it is the lighter's job to just make stunning visuals however he or she can. This chapter will explore the various ways materials and compositing can influence lighting.

Studio A Pipeline

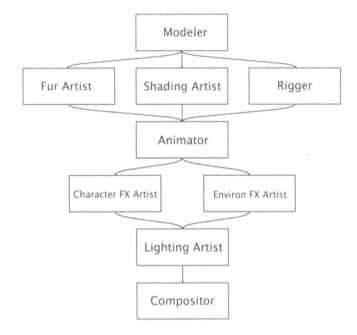

Studio B Pipeline

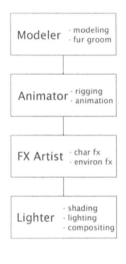

Figure 7.1 Different studios have uniquely different pipelines. Some require lighting artists to handle only the creation of lights while others require the lighter to be responsible for other tasks including shading and compositing.

Materials

The way any object in the world appears to the eye is a combination of the environment, the light sources, and the surface qualities of that object. The surface qualities of an object include the roughness, reflectivity, opacity, color, and a multitude of other nuanced variables that go into the appearance of the surface. It is these qualities that distinguish a piece of wood from metal from skin. Controlling and adjusting these attributes can give the artist the ultimate ability to adjust the look.

Surface Attributes

The overall appearance of a CG surface can be broken down into individual attributes designed to define their look. These attributes vary from object to object but most will be defined by some basic parameters. In a 3D work environment these attributes are given simple numeric values by default, but in most cases the artist will choose to create texture maps for each attribute. Texture maps are either images or procedural elements that are used to define these individual components.

Overall Color

The most basic attribute for any object is the overall color. This is the default color that lies on the surface of the object when illuminated by neutral light. Since most objects in the world are not one consistent color, texture maps or procedural maps are almost always used to represent the subtle variations that go into an object's overall color.

Figure 7.2 The sphere on the left has a procedural ramp applied to it while the one on the right has a painted texture map.

Specular Reflection or Specular Color

The specular reflection or specular color is the color of the highlights of the surface of the object. These highlights are a reflection of the light sources or bright objects in the scene.

A black specular color leaves the surface with no specularity at all while a white value leaves the highlight to mimic the same color as the light. When creating a texture map for the specular color it is important to remember this relationship. The whiter the area of the texture map, the more prominent the specular highlight in that region is when hit with light.

Figure 7.3 The sphere on the left has a procedural checkerboard applied to the specular attribute while the one on the right has a painted texture map. Both spheres show that the closer the map gets to a white value, the stronger the specular highlight.

Figure 7.4 There are many different types of reflection that a surface can create. Both images are from the animated short *Alarm* and property of MESAI.

Reflectivity/Reflected Color

Reflectivity is the object's ability to reflect the surrounding environment. Reflections occur whenever light hits an object. Therefore, almost all objects have some level of reflectivity. The amount and type of reflection are dependent on the light source and the object's surface material. The smoother the surface, the more reflective it is perceived to be. Smooth surfaces like chrome or mirrors will have a lot of perceived reflection while rougher surfaces like wool or raw tree bark will have very little to no perceived reflection.

Like specularity, the closer to white reflectivity becomes the more pronounced the object's reflection will be. A value of 0 or black will render no reflectivity. Additional setting for blur of the reflection and the reflective color exists as a way to fine tune the reflective look. These RGB values are multiplied by the main reflective value to ultimately determine the final look.

Bump/Displacement

Surfaces are rarely completely flat. Almost always, there is at least some subtle roughness to an object. The amount and shape of this roughness pattern can help distinguish objects such as metal or plastic or paper.

In CG, this attribute can be calculated in different ways. The two most popular are either bump mapping or displacement. The difference between these two attributes is that displacement offsets the geometry in the render and physically changes the surface of the object. Bump mapping, on the other hand, will only give the illusion of a textured surface by altering the surface normal of the object based on the map's value. The silhouette of the object will remain the same.

Unlike the other attributes discussed previously, these values are only driven by grayscale images. The more contrast in a particular region, the greater the bump or displacement offset will become.

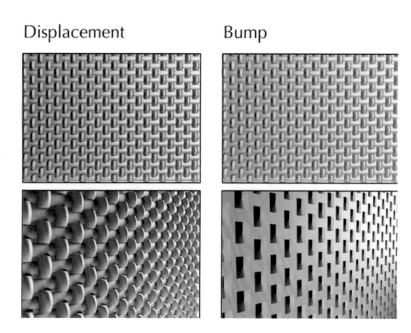

Displacement   Bump

Figure 7.5 The top row demonstrates that when an object is far away from the camera it may not matter if the artist uses displacement or bump. Once that image gets closer to the camera, the bump image begins to break down and a displacement map is needed.

Translucence

When an object is described as being translucent it means there is a certain amount of light that is able to pass through it. Translucency is different from transparency since light gets diffused to the point where objects on the other side are not clearly visible. Common translucent objects include leaves, sheets of paper, and flower petals. Accurately simulating translucence on these objects is essential to establishing their overall look.

Figure 7.6 Leaves are a great example of a translucent surface. Light is able to pass through the surface, but it is diffused enough so they are not considered transparent.

Incandescence

Incandescence is the visual appearance of an object glowing. It is almost like an inner fire that exists in the belly of an object and bursts out onto the environment. In CG, this simulates what the viewer would see when looking at an object like lava or a light bulb.

The one major thing to remember is that while adding incandescence can make an object appear as if it is emitting light, it may not affect the lighting of the surrounding objects unless some indirect illumination method in the renderer is activated.

Ambient Color

Ambient color is the color of the object without the addition of light. In other words, ambient light is what the object would look like if it existed in complete darkness. Most of the time, this setting will be left to black or very near it so an object will be properly shaded and fall into darkness when necessary. It is unnatural to have an object possess an ambient setting above 0 (black) because no object in reality can have a visible color without light. Therefore, this ambient color setting should be used sparingly if at all. Using it incorrectly could result in undesirable aesthetic results.

Figure 7.7 Examples of incandescent light. Stills from the animated short *Whole* and property of William Reynish.

Figure 7.8 Ambient color is the base color of an object before light of any kind is applied to it. *Pio* is downloadable character courtesy of Boutique23 (www.boutique23.com).

Simulating Specific Materials

It is easy to understand that artists need to look at objects in order to understand their surface attributes. It is much more difficult to know how to complete this analysis and what specific characteristics one should evaluate. This section will break down the surface attributes of real world objects to better understand that process and so it can be replicated in the future.

soft specular highlight   soft environment reflections   crisp environment reflections

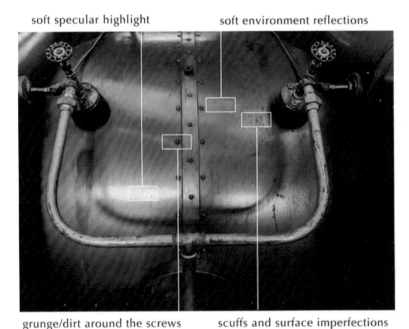

grunge/dirt around the screws   scuffs and surface imperfections   bright specular highlight

Figure 7.9 Breakdown of metal material.

old wood stain can cause color variations

circular splintering pattern

natural pattern of wood

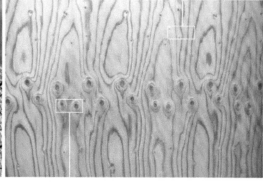

outdoor wood has weather damage

dead wood can get gray/desaturated

wood knot size/shape/clustering

Figure 7.10 Breakdown of wood material.

the denser the plastic, the less opaque

super bright specular highlight

reflection of surrounding objects

glancing angle of clear plastic looks black

rainbow pattern in specular highlights

shadow/spec change at the seam

Figure 7.11 Breakdown of plastic material.

specular highlight follows warped glass

reflection of window frame more intense than interior of room

highlight matches light color   thicker glass, more blurred refraction

window diffuses light and makes soft edges

Figure 7.12 Breakdown of window material.

wave/ripple relative size

caustic shape

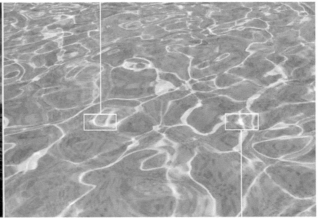

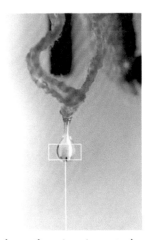

reflection of sun and sky

tight, bright specular highlights

droplet refraction inverted

Figure 7.13 Breakdown of water material.

light hits the surface before scattering in the interior and passing through the back

only goes darker after light passes through multiple surfaces

skin goes warm, reddish tone

Figure 7.14 Breakdown of sub-surface scattering material.

Common Adjustments to Shaders in Lighting

Rebalancing Materials

There are many complications that can arise in regard to shaders and materials once a shot is being lit. This can be a result of a large number of issues but often is caused by the different aspects of the shot not working together properly. In many instances there are a number of artists working on different models and shaders that, once combined, can look disjointed. The responsibility may fall on the lighter to rebalance the materials and shaders in order for the final image to be harmonious.

Ideally all the shaders in the same scene should be color balanced, but this is not always the case. If the lighting rig is blowing one area out but another area stays too dark this may be the case (see below). Running an omni test could provide the artist with the neccesary information(see below). If this is the case, it is often the best solution to go in and rebalance the materials. Look how much brighter the face is than the white shirt. This is a problem.

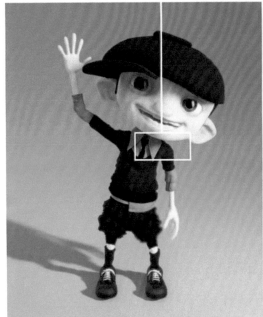

Render with Imbalanced Materials

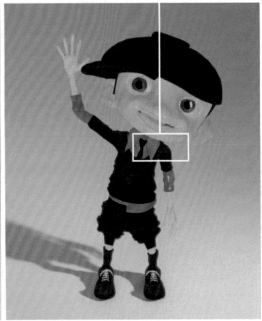

Omni Render

Figure 7.15 In this example, the white shirt appeared way too dark in comparison with the skin right next to it. After an omni render was done, it could be determined that the discrepancy in the material values is to blame. *Pio* is downloadable character courtesy of Boutique23 (www.boutique23.com).

This issue becomes apparent when lighting a shot where the light intensity that is working for one element is causing other objects to be either too bright or too dark. Ideally, the same key light with the same intensity would illuminate all objects uniformly. One way to solve this is through light linking and that is fine if the shot is worked on in isolation. This is not the best solution when working on an animated project with dozens or even hundreds of shots using the same materials and shaders. This can result in a very inefficient workflow of creating complex light rigs in every shot to counteract imbalanced materials. The better method is to rebalance the materials so they complement one another and then each subsequent shot requires a simpler light rig. This may take some extra time initially, but the long-term timesaving can be enormous.

One way to test for material balance is through an omni lighting test. If an artist creates an omni light casting no shadows with an intensity of 1, the artist can analyze the overall color of each object objectively. If any of the base materials are far out of line with the rest, they will appear in this test.

RGB Mattes with Material Files

Previously this book discussed creating layers for RGB mattes by assigning different shaders to different pieces of geometry. There are times, however, when an RGB matte will need to be created for a single piece of geometry. Say the artist wanted to make an RGB mask of a character's face in order to isolate the area around the nose and the area around the ears to do a special color modification or comp tweak. This is accomplished by creating a color matte that isolates the desired region in the red, green, or blue coloring. That material can then be applied to the object's ambient color value and all lights can be turned off in order to get the desired final image.

Figure 7.16 RGB mattes can be painted to isolate different sections of a single piece of geometry. *Pio* is downloadable character courtesy of Boutique23 (www.boutique23.com).

Compositing

Compositing is taking all the individually rendered elements and combining them in such a way as to create a beautiful final image. The major component of this process is properly layering all the rendered elements together so they make sense spatially and work together aesthetically. Does the character go in front of this tree or is he behind it? How are the diffuse renders combined with the specular renders? How are the RGB mattes controlled in the composite? Additionally, there are several common aesthetic adjustments that take place during the compositing process including color corrections, depth of field, light wrap, lens distortion, diffusion, and vignetting, to name a few.

Layering

What is an Alpha Channel?

An alpha channel is essentially a transparency mask that informs the image processing software where each calculation will take place. Most images rendered in a computer are designed to be composited together and have an alpha channel. This allows the different layers to identify their positive and negative space and allows them to merge together as anticipated.

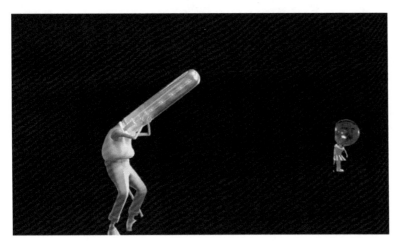

rgb channels

alpha channel

Figure 7.17 The alpha channel is a mask that isolates objects and helps determine the degree of transparency. In this example the objects have a white alpha, meaning they are opaque. The black regions of the image have a black alpha, meaning they will be 100 percent transparent if this image is laid over another.

Common Layering Methods

At its most basic level, compositing is a way to layer individual components together into one final image. This method goes as far back as the early days of animation when the common practice was Cel Animation. The Cel Animation process began with artists drawing separate elements of a shot on transparent acetate and then positioning those sheets beneath a camera to make it appear as though they were one image when photographed. This method allowed the static parts to be the same image from frame to frame while only animating the layers that contained the character or object that was moving. If the character was bouncing around but the background was stationary then only the image containing the character would need to be redrawn.

There are many different ways two images can be layered together in modern digital compositors. Many of these methods use the same principles as Cel Animation while others are completely

Figure 7.18 An example of the Cel Animation stills used on Disney's *The Little Mermaid.* © Disney.

digital concepts. Some may be used more than others, but each has its place and should be understood for its individual merits.

The most basic layering concept in digital compositing is exactly the same as Cel Animation. Just take one image and put it over another. In digital compositing, this is done by using an "over" node. In the example in Figure 7.19, the red square is being layered over the blue square. The "over" node is probably used more than any other layering node. It is commonly implemented when layering beauty layers together or simply combining various elements to the shot.

The "plus" (or "minus") merge operation is a mathematical way to combine layers. Instead of placing one image over the other, the "plus" operation merges the two images together by adding the RGB values together. If one has a red channel value of 0.50 and the other is 0.25, then the resulting image will have a red value of 0.75 (0.25 + 0.50). This is repeated for each channel and that is how the final image is created.

When a pure red square is merged using the plus operation with a pure blue square, the result is magenta. A less obvious combination is when red combines with green, as in Figure 7.19. The resulting image is yellow, which seems to go against logic. If red and green paint were combined, the result would definitely not be yellow. This is because the way light combines is very different

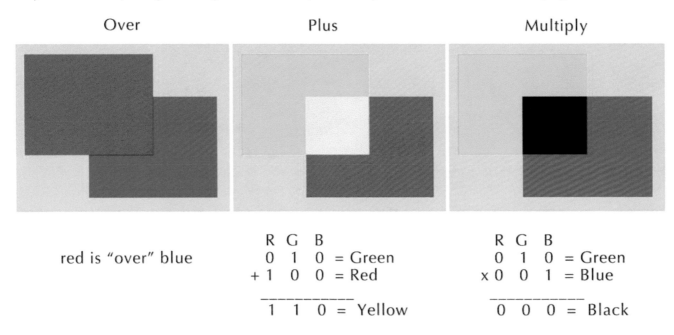

	Over	Plus	Multiply

red is "over" blue

```
R  G  B
0  1  0  = Green
+ 1  0  0  = Red
_____
1  1  0  = Yellow
```

```
R  G  B
0  1  0  = Green
x 0  0  1  = Blue
_____
0  0  0  = Black
```

Figure 7.19 Examples of the "over," "plus," and "multiple" operations merging colors together.

from physical colors in the real world. So it is important for artists to fully analyze the mathematical implications when considering color combinations.

A production example of using the "plus" operation is combining different light passes. Say the artist decides to render each light separately and combine them in the comp to have greater control. These rendered elements should not be combined by using the "over" operation because that will give a false result. Instead, the artist will use the "plus" operation to add all these different light passes together to simulate the nature of adding light to a scene.

"Multiply" is another mathematical operation similar to "plus." Instead of adding values, the "multiply" operation will multiply the channels together to create the resulting image. Take the same example as before. Instead of the resulting image being yellow, it is actually black. This is because of the idea that if any number is multiplied by 0 the resulting number is 0.

In that way, the "multiply" operation is a bit counterintuitive. Normally multiplying numbers increases their values. But in computer graphics, multiplying will normally darken the image since RGB values normally range from 0 to 1, and multiplying a number by less than 1 will actually decrease its value.

A common use of this operation is when dealing with shadow and ambient occlusion passes. Both shadow and ambient occlusion passes are mostly white with the areas being affected as darker. When these images are multiplied into the original image, the resulting image is properly darkened in the shadowed areas and left at their original values in the white regions.

"Screen" works in a way that is the inverse of "multiply." Unlike "multiply," which generally darkens an image, "screen" merges will

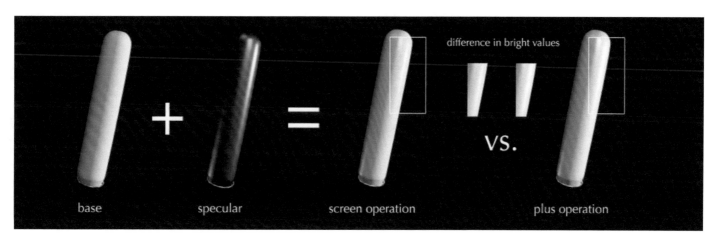

Figure 7.20 Comparing "screen" vs. "plus" when adding a specular pass.

brighten the image. "Screen" gets its name from a real world lighting phenomenon. This phenomenon is simulating the effect of combining two separate slide images on one screen and seeing the resulting image.

The major benefit of using "screen" is that it will raise the midtones of the image without affecting the dark areas or pushing the bright areas beyond a value of 1. One example of using the "screen" operation in a production environment is to create a pass to add some additional specularity to an image. If the artist uses the "plus" operation, the added specular values could combine with the original image to leave areas too bright.

There are many other layering methods that will be used over the course of an animated project, but the ones described here are the most common. Ultimately the artist just needs to be aware that each merge function has a different mathematical or theoretical basis for the operation and, by understanding those facets, he or she can have more control of the final image.

Color Corrections

After properly layering all the necessary rendered elements together, the artist now has the opportunity to start making color correction or adjustments to an image. This tweaking of colors represents a huge portion of the artist's time. Whether it is perfecting a character's skin tone or pushing the values of the color of the tree trunks just a bit more to match the previous shot, these types of tweaks will make a huge difference in the final image. There are several basic ways of adjusting colors that are available in any compositing software package. Having an understanding of each will go a long way in giving the artist the ultimate control over color of the scene.

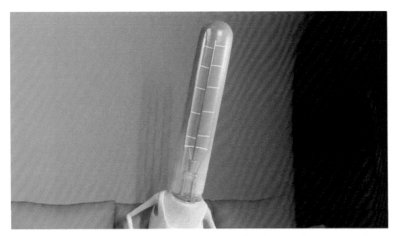

before color correction

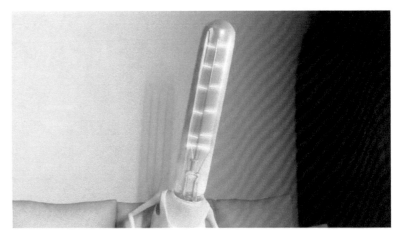

after color correction

Figure 7.21 Example of how subtle color corrections and value tweaks can improve an image and make it more dynamic.

Gamma

Modifying the color of an image by influencing the gamma is most useful when attempting to adjust the midtones. The darks and lights values of an image will remain relatively the same when gamma corrections are made, but the largest changes happen in the middle values. If it is thought of in terms of a color graph, the gamma would be adding a point to the middle of the curve and bending it upward or downward, but the top and bottom are pinned to 0 and 1. This is demonstrated in the graph in Figure 7.22.

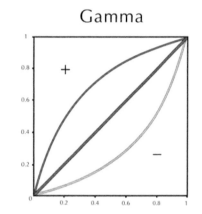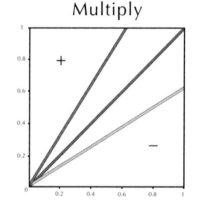

Figure 7.22 Gamma and multiply color correction graphs.

Multiply

Multiplying the RGB values of an image is exactly what it sounds like. Take a gray pixel with RGB values of 0.5 0.5 0.5. If those three values are multiplied by 1.5, then the resulting image is a gray image with a brighter RGB value of 0.75 0.75 0.75.

The result of this process is that images have higher contrast as values are multiplied to brighten and less contrast as they decrease the brightness. To exemplify this, take these two pixels side by side. One is almost black with values of 0.1 0.1 0.1. The pixel next to it is middle gray with 0.5 0.5 0.5. If the colors are multiplied by 2, the results are that the gray pixel becomes white (1 1 1) and the dark pixel becomes

0.2 0.2 0.2. The difference in value between the two pixels has increased from 0.4 to 0.8 and the result is that the image has gained contrast.

Multiplication works for colors as well. Each channel multiplies together to get the final RGB value. If, for example, an artist wanted to take something white and make it red, the artist would take the white layer and multiply it by a red color (1 x 1,1 x 0,1 x 0 = 1,0,0). Or if the artist multiplied a cyan image by a magenta image (1 x 0,0 x 1,1 x 1 = 0,0,1) the result would be blue.

Color Corrections with Alpha

Of course there are times when an artist wants to manipulate only a section of the image. In order to do that, the artist must manipulate the alpha channel of the color correction. This can be done in a multiple number of ways, but two of the most common are isolating an area with a roto and utilizing render mattes.

Using a roto is fairly straightforward. The roto allows the artist the ability to draw a region on the screen where the color correction or alteration can take place. Rotos are great in some circumstances, but can be problematic if either the area being adjusted is being animated or the camera is moving. This would mean that the roto would need to be animated and this could cause some arduous work for the artist.

Another method of controlling color is through using rendered mattes (previously discussed in Chapter 4). These mattes are created at the time of render and can be used in the alpha channel to isolate particular elements in the shot. These are great when the artist wants to make color tweaks in the composite to the shoes of a character or the shutters on a house. The best part about these types of mattes is that they are a perfect pixel-to-pixel match on every frame even when there is animation, motion blur, or camera moves.

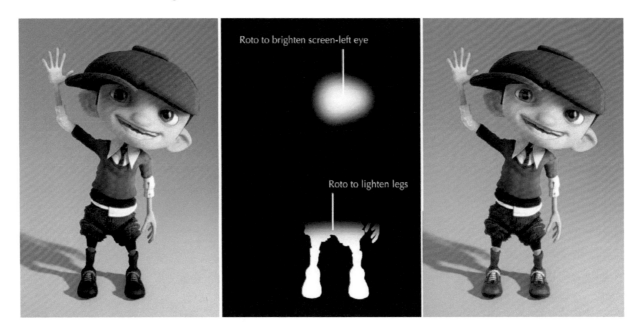

Figure 7.23 Rotoshapes can be used alone or combined with matte passes to make color corrections. *Pio* is downloadable character courtesy of Boutique23 (**www.boutique23.com**).

The Final Touches

There are some additional visual cues that are added in the composite that add that extra bit of believability and touches that can make an image come alive. These are not always large-scale changes that are obvious to the audience, but instead very minor tweaks that just make an image "feel right."

Edge Blur/Light Wrap

One of the biggest factors that can make a CG image "feel wrong" is crisp edges and perfect corners. A small but important element when making a CG image feel more natural is edge blur and light wrap. These are at the points where one piece of geometry comes into contact with another piece of geometry in the 2D image. If a photograph or even human vision is analyzed, it is clear that when one object is in front of the other, there is a tiny bit where these two objects' color and value merge together. Even in the most crisp, precise photographs there is still a bit of edge softness that will always occur in the world.

Naturally, when compositing layered renders together this element is not automatically present. One object is slapped over the other and there is a hard line of distinction between the two elements. This difference is too harsh and perceived by the audience almost immediately as being false and incorrect.

The solution is to create a bit of edge blur. Edge blur involves isolating the outer edge of an object (an edge detect operation is commonly used for this) and giving those areas a 1–3 pixel blur in

Figure 7.24 Edge blur and light wrap add softness to the outline of an object and are especially important when an object is against a very bright background as in these examples. Still from the animated short *The Fantastic Flying Books of Mr. Morris Lessmore*. Property of Moonbot Studios **(right)**.

order to make the entirety of the image come together. Be careful not to use this too heavily since too much edge blur can look equally incorrect to the audience.

In some instances, this needs to be taken a step further. Whenever an object is between the camera and a very bright background, light wrapping will occur. This is the bright element seeping around the sides of the foreground element. Take a sunset, for example. If a character or object is standing in between that bright sun and the camera, the color and value of the sun will wrap around the edges of the foreground element and become visible. To replicate this look, the artist should take a similar edge detect and isolate the colors and values of the background in that area. If blurred slightly and layered back over the top of the foreground element, a very effective replication of natural light wrap occurs.

Diffusion

This softening of the image occurs not only on the edges and outer components of an image, but also the inside of the objects. This is especially true of bright, sunlit areas and specular highlights. In those areas the optics of a camera, or the human eye for that matter, can get a bit fuzzy and cause these areas to appear soft. The solution is to isolate the brighter regions of an image and blur those areas slightly. Obviously, this blur is minor and not meant to cause the object itself to go out of focus. This is just a few pixels to give the CG image a more lifelike feeling. Depending on the desired mood, the effect of diffusion can be increased or exaggerated past the natural level to generate emotion from the audience.

without diffusion

with diffusion

Figure 7.25 Example of a photograph with and without diffusion.

Vignetting

As described in previous chapters, vignetting is normally a slight darkening of the edges of the frame to help the audience focus their attention on the central elements. Often, this is done in the render and with the use of spotlights. There are times, however, when this effect can be done with a 2D solution in the composite. It is generally just a blurred roto used around the edge of the frames to bring down the values slightly.

There are some obstacles to be aware of when creating a vignette. These obstacles center on avoiding exposure of this effect to the audience. The first issue is not to make the vignetting too dark and obvious to the audience. Also, be careful when the camera is moving. In those circumstances the darkening around the edge of the frame can be obvious and can also break the illusion. The other major issue is the darkening of very bright areas. These can make them looked clamped and flat. Therefore, a nice, subtle, soft vignette is normally ideal.

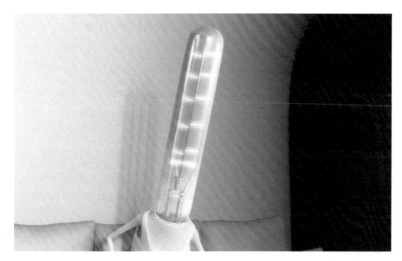

without vignette

with vignette

Figure 7.26 Example of an image with and without vignetting.

Lens Effects

In live action films and photography there are artifacts that occur when a camera faces directly into the light. Depending on the lens, the type of light, and the film being used or digital capture, these artifacts appear to be quite different. Sometimes when shooting in the natural world these are accidents and sometimes they are aesthetically designed to be in the shot. Either way, they are an expected occurrence when shooting directly into sunlight or another extremely bright light source.

Often, compositing software has the ability to simulate this effect. There are different shapes and styles of lens effects the artist can choose from. The one major thing to remember when using lens effects is that it is actually happening inside the lens. So even though the light source may be behind certain elements, the flare needs to be comped over everything else in order for it to appear correct.

Lens effects have a negative connotation with some artists if used too often. They can be said to look gimmicky and be a cheap way of adding interest to a shot. Therefore, it is wise to use lens effects sparingly and tactfully.

Figure 7.27 The sun and other bright light sources can cause an optical effect in a camera's lens known as a lens flare.

Depth of Field

Depth of field has been discussed in previous chapters as a fantastic adjustment which mimics a photographic anomaly and can focus the viewer's eye on the desired region. Depth of field is generally applied in the composite, and when that occurs the artist can have complete control over the look. One control is the ability to animate the focal point. This focal point can also be changed over the course of the shot to direct the audience's eye to multiple story points. This is referred to as "racking" focus. There may be characters in the foreground discussing something and the attention needs to shift to action in the background.

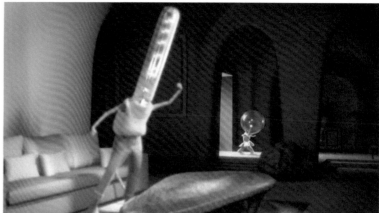

Figure 7.28 In the left image the grandfather is the focal point, but by racking the focus onto the girl the audience is more likely to concentrate on her.

How Depth of Field is Created

Most render software programs offer the ability to add depth of field during the render. The user can identify a focal point and instruct the renderer how far in front or behind that point to render in focus. Renderers can also give controls that are similar to a physical camera that determine the depth of field based on these simulated settings.

That being said, it is very rare for an animated project to rely on the rendering software for depth of field. Almost always the blurring caused by depth of field is added in the compositor. The main reason for this is the quick turnaround in the compositor versus the renderer. In the render, the artist will modify the settings, hit render, and often wait for long periods of time before seeing any results. This is especially problematic when working with shots that require a rack focus. Any tweak would be made and the artist could wait hours or days for a long render of many layers and many frames to complete.

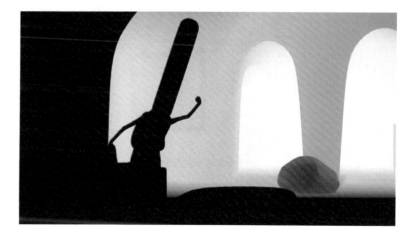

Figure 7.29 Example of a z-depth render.

The solution is to generate a z-depth pass (or z-map) in the renderer and use that to manipulate the depth of field in the compositor. A z-depth pass is a grayscale, visual representation of the depth. Normally, the closer an object is to the camera the whiter it is while more distant objects are darker. This grayscale image can be used to create the areas of defocus in front of or behind the center of focus and simulate depth of field.

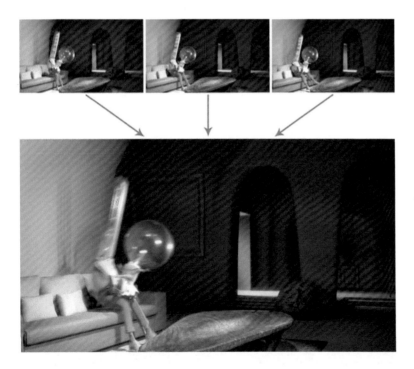

Figure 7.30 By successfully implementing a 2D motion blur solution, the artist can potentially save hours of render time.

2D Motion Blur

Enabling motion blur in a render can make movements flow together smoothly, but it can also increase the render time significantly. In some instances, this increase can cause a project to go past its deadline and a solution in the compositor is required. The solution is using one of the many 2D motion blur plug-ins that exist. There are a variety of methods that can generate 2D motion blur, but generally they first look at a single frame and analyze some of the frames surrounding it. If an object is moving between those frames, the compositing software will interpolate the movement between those points with a blurred image essentially mimicking the look of motion blur. Although this is not a flawless method and can cause problems in a number of situations, as when characters or objects come on and off screen and when there is a lot of movement, there are definitely times when using this method can cut down on render times substantially.

Reducing Noise/Chatter

One of the biggest pains for a lighting or rendering artist can be noise or chatter. This is caused by insufficient samples or resolution when rendering and the visual outcome is an image that appears gritty or grainy. When multiple frames are rendered for an animated shot, these gritty areas of the image can flicker like film grain and make the image appear "noisy."

As discussed previously, common solutions are to increase render settings or to increase the image size. An additional, timesaving solution can be done just by adding some nodes in the compositing software. This method is called frame blending. It is similar

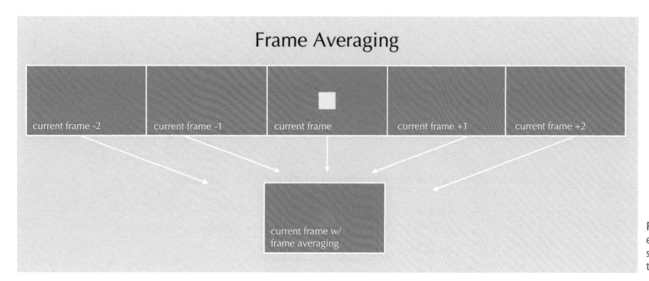

Figure 7.31 Frame averaging helps eliminate noise and chatter by sampling from surrounding frames to normalize the image.

to 2D motion blur in that the compositor will take samples within a given region from surrounding frames and average the pixels together to make a more consistent value. Say, for example, over the course of five frames a pixel has the following values in one of the channels: 0.5, 0.8, 0.7, 0.6, 0.5. The result of frame averaging is to make a pixel with a value of 0.62. This averaging can greatly reduce or even eliminate the noise in certain instances. The biggest downside to this method is that it can only be used on stationary or slow-moving objects. If the camera is moving quickly, the frame averaging is sampling too wide a variety of pixels and will just appear blurry. Not all compositing software has this option, but if it does exist it is a useful tool for the CG lighter.

Final Thoughts

Being a lighter is not solely understanding and manipulating lights. It is about taking 3D geometry and making an image that comes alive. That means that lighters need to have full understanding and control of materials and compositing in order to meet that goal.

Many young artists make the assumption that there is an army of other artists at every company that will create the material attributes and composite the shot for the lighter. In many cases, nothing could be further from the truth. The lighting artist's job description can include painting texture maps, building shaders, creating final composites, and everything in between. Remember, the ultimate role of the lighting artist is to make a beautiful final image. The more understanding and control the artist can have over the image, the more likely he or she will be able to achieve that goal.

Interview
with Brian Hill

Supervisor of the Materials Department :: Blue Sky Studios.

Q. What is your current job/role at your company?
A. I am currently the Supervisor of the Materials Department at Blue Sky Studios.

Q. What inspired you to become an artist on CG films?
A. I originally started out as a mechanical engineering major in college. By the time I graduated I had decided that strict engineering really wasn't for me, but I was really interested in the technical/software side of it (FEA, CAD, etc.), so I went to work for a 3D CAD company (SolidWorks) for a few years. I started off doing technical support and while I was there I got involved in the development and testing of their photorealistic rendering plug-in PhotoWorks on the side. Being able to not only model something in the computer in 3D, but also visualize it in a semi-photorealistic way was really mind-blowing for me. That was really the turning point for me. From then on I had my eyes set on getting into CG one way or another.

Q. What non-CG artwork inspires you?
A. Metal sculpture. I love it. In my final year of college, I took a metal sculpting class to help break up my engineering load, and it was amazing.

Q. What are some of the specific skills you look for when reviewing a demo reel?

A. When hiring for a materials TD position here at Blue Sky we always look at the reels first. At the end of the day our job is to put pretty pictures up on the screen—so we tend the vet the reels first on aesthetics. Are the images appealing? Are they "different" than the usual classroom tutorials? Does the artist have full control over all aspects of the material (color, specularity, bump, translucency, etc.)?

The job of a materials TD at Blue Sky can be a very technical one at times, so if they pass the first check then we try and find out more about exactly how they made the image. What techniques did they employ? Was everything hand painted, tiled texture maps, or were some elements of the image created procedurally? Did they have to write any scripts or tools to help throughout the process to get the job done?

Q. What is the most important aspect of creating materials for a character?

A. I always try and make sure that my team focuses on the eyes, face, and head. The vast majority of the time that is where the audience is going to be looking.

After that—hands and feet.

Additionally, making sure that the character fits into the style of the world and works well next to the other characters in the show is very important. Usually the character part of our pipeline happens well before the set and sequence part, so we don't have actual production shots to work with. At that point I'll often ask the team to prepare some side-by-side comparisons of characters that will act alongside each other in the film. That way the art director and director can get a feeling for however they will work together in the shot.

Q. When you are working with a large set, where do you begin? Do you develop rough shaders for all objects and then refine or do you work on each asset until completion?

A. It tends to vary a little show to show, but we usually approach sets with a multi-pass approach. Coverage pass first, then review with the art director and, depending on the film, possibly the director as well. Once we have their notes and a rough idea of what parts of the set are important to them and to telling the story, we'll go back in and detail those areas first, and then increase the detail on the rest of the set as time permits to make sure it all works together as a whole.

On some shows, particularly those that are a "new world" for us (not a sequel), we'll usually try and approach the new vegetation first in isolation, working back and forth with the art director to usually a medium detail pass. Then once we see the vegetation in the set, we'll go in and do refinements as needed.

Q. The company you work for uses a lot of procedural materials. What are some of the benefits of that workflow versus painted textures?

A. In most cases, no UV layouts are needed—and you're not tied to the topology, so topology changes can happen without a materials artist having to go back and redo or transfer work.

Faster tweaks to elements within the material.

"Plop-and-drop" material libraries that we can use to quickly block out a rough pass on a sequence or set.

Pre-programmed randomization can be built into material libraries so the same material applied to different assets can have different looks right out of the box (random color shifts, noise scales, etc.)

Q. What's the one sequence or shot you are most proud to have worked on?

A. I have to pick just one?! That's going to be tough. As a materials TD, my favorite work was some of the first work I did at Blue Sky on *Robots*. I didn't get to work on too many sets or sequences as most of those had already been built up by the time I started, but I did get to work on quite a few characters and props. That movie was a materials TD's dream—we had so much freedom to make everything dirty, scratched up and 'used' looking. One of the ones I remember the most was the "battle armor" for some of the lead characters as they suit up for the final battle at the end of the film.

Q. In your opinion, what makes a good shading artist?

A. It is someone that has a good artistic eye, who is technically sound, and constantly looking at the world around them wondering how they would make that material.

Q. If you could tell yourself one piece of advice when you were first starting out in this industry, what would it be?

A. Sometimes we can all get caught up in making something into the best we want it to be in our own eyes. Always make sure to look at the film you're creating from the point of view of the audience. Everything you do should be geared toward making them enjoy watching your work, over and over and over.

 8

Honing the Artistic Eye

Up to this point, this book has focused on the individual elements that make up a well-lit shot. We have discussed character lighting and point lights and compositing and RGB mattes as separate elements. In reality, these elements do not work in isolation but instead in coordination with one another to create an overall look. In this chapter, the goal is to focus on successful shots in animated films and how each utilized the techniques discussed in previous chapters to create beautiful images.

The shaping on these puppies allows the audience to read each one individually and so they are seen as a massive cluster of individuals inside the larger mass.

This shot shows a struggle between life and death. Yellows and greens represent the sections of life while cool blues and whites represent death. The cool, screen-left tree is adding to this feeling of cool death by highlighting the sharp, jagged tree branches. Conversely, the soft, rounded shapes of the screen-right tree are being hit with warmer light.

Each character also sits over a dark section of background, which allows their bright values to pop off the dark background. Notice how his face is slightly brighter than the rest of his body so it reads more clearly and the audience's eye is drawn to it.

A gobo type look to the ground plane to give a sense of scale. It also works in this instance to add some texture and surface definition.

The characters are nicely rimmed allowing the audience to distinguish their shapes despite being small on the screen.

She sits in a perfect circle surrounding her. The light on the trunk of the tree and hanging leaves behind her create a perfect frame for the audience to focus on her.

Figure 8.1 Still from the animated short *Premier Automne*. Property of Carlos DeCarvalho.

The artist is using the existence of an off screen-left fireplace to create a subtle rim on the screen-left side of the character's face to help define his outline.

Notice the eye dings in this shot. This is an excellent example of using the existing elements within a scene to create a believable specular highlight in the eyes that gives the character life and a soul without being an artificially added perfect circle.

The light falloff from the candle gives this scene a natural vignette and keeps the viewer's attention in the center of the screen.

There is some beautiful shaping in this scene with the soft roll-off of values across almost every object in the scene. The cake, the table, the face, the pot, and the hat all have a variation in values away from the main light source.

Figure 8.2 Still from the animated short *Little Freak*. Property of Edwin Schaap.

The focal point of this shot is clearly the candle. It is the brightest area on screen and all areas darken as the viewer's eye moves away from that point.

The audience can absolutely believe that the main key light hitting all the objects in the scene is emanating from the candle. More than likely though, the artist used the physical position of that candle as only a general location for all the lights in the scene. In reality the candle would probably light the top of the cake more evenly and flatten out the character's face a bit more since the illumination is so frontal. Instead, the artist adjusted those positions to get the very successful shaping we are seeing.

The gobo is serving multiple functional purposes in this shot. One, it is creating visual interest in what otherwise would be a visually flat door. Two, it is implying a much larger space. This gobo shows characters walking past and a flood of activity. In reality, it is just an illusion because we never actually see that part of the set in this short. Finally, it creates a nice area of shadow for the character to sit upon and pop off from the background.

It is also important to note the large specular shape on the rounded "knob" on the door. Highlights such as this can be added to inject much needed dimensionality and variation to a region.

The complementary colors of the warm, pink character against the cooler green door allows him to pop off from the background.

Figure 8.3 Still from the animated short *Shave It*. Property of 3DAR.

The key illumination creates an interesting situation. For Edmund (the man) the key light is working as a rim and allowing his back to go darker. Since the light is striking his face, his reflection is much brighter which is exactly what the artist wants since reading the reflection of the donkey is the most important story element of this shot. The very cool, desaturated, industrial look adds to the feelings of isolation and confusion the character is feeling at this point in the film.

The glow around the fluorescent lights also does a great job of integrating those light sources into the space.

Square objects like the lockers or the sink can be difficult to get good shaping on, but this artist does a brilliant job by creating horizontal variation, but also vertical variation that makes these objects come alive.

This shot has fantastic visual shaping around the set and the creation of a natural vignette which successfully frames the characters.

Figure 8.4 Still from the animated short *The Fantastic Flying Books of Mr. Morris Lessmore*. Property of Moonbot Studios.

Notice the areas around the windows and doorways where the interior meets the exterior brightness. The edges where those two areas meet are blurred making a successful integration between the two spaces. If these areas had hard edges, the whole scene would feel like two separate spaces.

The lighting artist also took time to specifically light elements in the scene with great care. Pay attention to the foreground, screen-left globe. This set piece is definitely beautifully lit with a strong key light from an off-screen window and is artistically crafted. There is a nicely placed rim light and subtle variation throughout the entire object.

This scene does a nice job of showcasing the difference that can sometimes occur between exposures for the interior versus exterior lighting. This shot is exposed for the interior and the artist chose to make the resulting exterior appear pure white without the viewer being able to read any exterior elements like trees or buildings.

Figure 8.5 Still from the animated short *Edmond était un âne* (Edmond was a Donkey). Property of Papy3d/ONF NFB/ARTE.

The artist does a great job of creating dark values around the edges essentially creating a vignette to keep the viewer's attention on the character in the middle of the frame.

This secondary light is also a major element used in creating visual shaping. Notice how the areas closer to where the key light hits receive more bounce light and it slowly fades down as the space gets further away. The darkest areas are in the corners of the room. Also notice the vertical variation on the walls. In other words: the subtle lessening of the bounce's influence as the viewer looks along the wall. All the variation creates successful visual shaping in all areas of the room not influenced directly by the key.

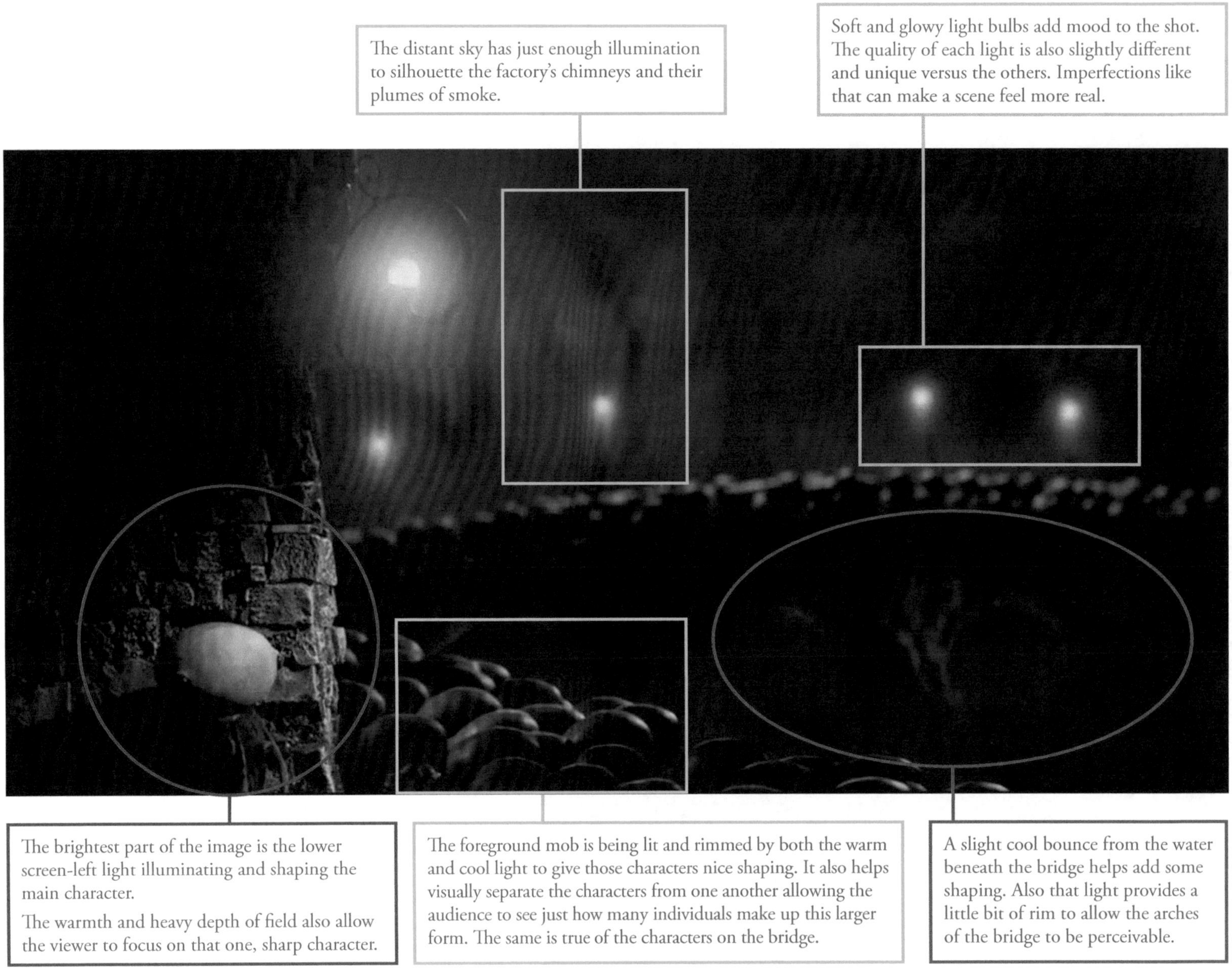

The distant sky has just enough illumination to silhouette the factory's chimneys and their plumes of smoke.

Soft and glowy light bulbs add mood to the shot. The quality of each light is also slightly different and unique versus the others. Imperfections like that can make a scene feel more real.

The brightest part of the image is the lower screen-left light illuminating and shaping the main character.

The warmth and heavy depth of field also allow the viewer to focus on that one, sharp character.

The foreground mob is being lit and rimmed by both the warm and cool light to give those characters nice shaping. It also helps visually separate the characters from one another allowing the audience to see just how many individuals make up this larger form. The same is true of the characters on the bridge.

A slight cool bounce from the water beneath the bridge helps add some shaping. Also that light provides a little bit of rim to allow the arches of the bridge to be perceivable.

Figure 8.6 Images from *Cicada Princess* used by permission courtesy of Mauricio Baiocchi ©2014 Mauricio Baiocchi. Portions © Steven Ferrara. Lighting Artist Yun Shin.

The screen-left rim on the bear is not necessarily from a known light source, but it is a nice detail to help the audience identify him from the background images.

The artist's addition of a hint of reflection in the black circle to give just a touch of shaping and value is very clever.

The shaping across the character's robotic head from key to fill side is extremely subtle and well done.

Figure 8.7 Still from the animated short *L3.0*. Property of Pierre Jury, Vincent Defour, Cyril Declercq, Alexis Decelle, and ISART DIGITAL (school).

The floor has fantastic variation from the bright window off screen right to the darker screen-left side. Also, the desaturated reds and blues on the floor definitely make the room feel dusty and worn.

The atmospheric effects not only add scale and depth to the scene, they also desaturate and cool the rock behind the background character which allows his warmer tones to pop off the screen.

The camera position allows the legs of the foreground character to frame the background character nicely.

The foreground character is darker tonally to allow the audience to focus on the giant man coming toward the camera. Notice though, how the dark sneakers of the foreground character do not go completely black. The artist adds a little value to these objects to give a tiny bit of shaping and to keep them from becoming a flat black.

The soft vignetting keeps the viewer's eye on the center of the screen.

Figure 8.8 Still from the animated short *Mac and Cheese*. Property of Colorbleed Animation Studio.

The eye's sclera is cranked up to make sure to get a good eye read. The eyes also have a softer reflection of the environment to give the character some life.

The heavy depth of field allows the audience to focus specifically on the character's face to understand his emotion through his facial expression.

The dirt and decay on this character's teeth do a great job of establishing him as a tough and gritty man.

This is beautiful character lighting. There is fantastic shaping not only on the character's face but also his hands, his arm, his hammer, and his shirt.

Figure 8.9 © 2010 Ubisoft Entertainment. All Rights Reserved. *Raving Rabbids Travel In Time*, Ubisoft and the Ubisoft logo are trademarks of Ubisoft Entertainment in the U.S. and/or other countries. Trailer produced by Akama. All other rights are reserved by Ubisoft Entertainment.

Interview
with Gabriel Portnof

CG Supervisor and Previz :: Dreamworks Animation

Q. What is your current job/role at your company?
A. I am currently a CG Supervisor at DreamWorks Animation. I am responsible for delivering full film sequences through surfacing, lighting, compositing, paint fix, and finally to luster. I manage mid- to large-size teams of lighting artists and technical directors. I show these movie sequences to the VFX supervisor, production designer, art director, director, and finally the executive studio management before it goes to film.

Q. What inspired you to become an artist on CG films?
A. I have always been a fan of animation and VFX from childhood. Since I could hold a pencil, I have also always been a painter and very much involved in the arts. I have worked in all mediums from chalk, oil paints, to spray paint while doing graffiti murals ... I grew up in NYC so it was very much a part of my culture. But after college I needed to work and find a way to make steady money. Painting murals and selling my work really didn't appeal to me as I wanted to keep all of it to myself and not sell anything. I started on my current path in magazine graphics learning image manipulation using programs like Photoshop and After Effects on old Macintosh clones. That became a bit boring and repetitive technically and it failed to really challenge me. I eventually decided to get a Masters of Fine Art from SVA in NYC to really learn 3D/motion graphics/film making. After that I worked in advertising and video game cinematics for a few years at various places like R/GA and Blur. But really, what I wanted to do was the high-end feature films because of how large-scale and polished they are. Eventually my reel became good enough for DreamWorks and they moved me to San Francisco to light for *Shrek 2*.

Q. What non-CG artwork inspires you?

A. I grew up blocks from the Metropolitan Museum of Art and the MOMA so there are literally thousands of paintings, photos, and sculptures that move me. I was a huge fan of Red Groomes after seeing his piece *Ruckus Manhattan* ... which was a large-scale paper maché version of Manhattan in the 70s. I also love Rembrandt and any artist who really tries to capture light. Basically, all of the artists in the Hudson Valley School, and most Impressionists. My paintings and artwork always were a study in lighting of some kind or another. It made sense that my professional life focused on this too. I could go on for hours about art and lighting. It's what motivates all the decisions I have made to get to this job and the images I make doing this job.

Q. Can you talk us through your process of critiquing an image for its positives and negatives?

A. Generally it's always a case-by-case basis. Ask yourself, "What's the point of the shot or sequence or frame?" If it's a specific mood then you can go with the usual color choices. Cool tones for calmness, depression, sadness, seriousness. Warm tones for anger, conflict, or even comfort if the warmth is not too red. General rule of thumb for feature film lighting is to be sure you are helping the story out. Are you putting emphasis to the action or character? Are you de-emphasizing areas that aren't important? You also have to make sure you aren't being too complex or distracting. Most of the time the director wants the film to be pretty but his/her real interest is the story they are trying to tell. Really good lighting is the kind of lighting you *don't* notice.

Q. Visually, what is the most important element in a successful image for an animated film?

A. The story is the most important element. The lighting has to tell the story, it has to help the moment get conveyed to the audience. A successfully lit frame shouldn't scream "Look at the pretty lighting!!!" It should of course be pretty, but it shouldn't have a presence so the audience stops to look at it instead of following the story of the film. It should fit perfectly into the moment so as to almost go unnoticed. Remember that most directors are storytellers and not artists. Their job is to tell the story without too much distraction. Audiences are also not usually so tuned into the nuances of light and color as their emotions are. They also want to like or hate the characters, they want to understand the action. All too often lighting and action can hinder this in that they try too hard to make everything beautiful. If you light and color an element in the background so dramatically and beautifully, you can actually harm the film when the audience ends up looking in the wrong part of the frame and missing the acting or the action. But don't get me wrong, light all those elements as well as you can, but when compositing use depth of field and make sure the attention and focus of the image will always be where it needs to be. These images fly by at 1/24th or 1/48th of a second and people need to be told where and what to look at without hesitation.

Q. What do you think is lighting's largest contribution to an animated film?

A. I think it's one of the most important parts of a film that people are unaware of. Most people won't even think about it, especially if it's done right. But ... when they are in the moment, looking at beautiful colorful and sometimes photo-realistic images, and they really feel it's real ... and they are in the moment ... that's when lighting is truly contributing to the film. Fans will speak of their favorite characters, and their favorite plot twists, but what they see in their minds is actually the lighting. What they remember most vividly is the rich images that the movie takes place within. Lighting doesn't get the fame and the glory, there isn't even an award for lighting at the Annie Awards ... but imagine if these movies weren't lit? Have you ever watched a film pre-lighting? Shaded simply by OpenGL shaders? It's hard to know what to look at. Nothing looks real, and it doesn't have any shape to it that makes physical sense. It's hard to know how to feel. It is very much missing the flavor of the final lighting images. What lighting adds to the film is immeasurable and is hard to quantify. A film without lighting is like corn flakes without the milk.

Q. Where do you think the future of lighting is headed?

A. Lighting has always been headed to photo-realism in both animation and VFX. Every software innovation since the beginning has been to harness the ever growing power of the processor to fake what happens to light in real life. When I started we had to fake bounce lighting with point lights, and soft shadows of any kind were super expensive. Now we have global illumination, radiosity, gathering, and occlusion as normal tools, even for the single computer user at home on a PC. MCRT renderers like Arnold are bringing physically based rendering to small shops and taking a lot of the labor out of lighting and allowing artists to spend their newfound time to polish and make real artistic decisions. I think like all things it's slowly taking the labor out of the task ... but that being said, lighting will never be fully automated for storytelling. Just because it is getting easier to make things look pretty and real doesn't mean an artist isn't needed to manipulate that real lighting to fit the composition or story or mood of the film. Even though MCRT makes soft ray-traced shadows and bounce lighting out of the box doesn't mean directors want what's accurate. They will want artistic manipulation and choices to be made to further the story they are telling. They will want stylized looks and maybe even intentionally not realistic-looking images. Lighting is an art and a necessity to filmmaking.

Q. If you could tell yourself one piece of advice when you were first starting out in this industry, what would it be?

A. Try a little bit of everything before making big decisions. I was a generalist at first and I think it was a good move since I know how to do everything from modeling, animation, FX, lighting, surfacing, and compositing ... even editing and storyboarding. I would tell myself not to make a hard decision about narrowing it down to join a big studio too soon. I made a thesis in school but I should have done more on my own. I feel that once you join the workforce, you lose that ability to make something totally your own. That's the sweet spot of animation. Doing it for yourself.

Q. In your opinion, what makes a good lighting artist?

A. I used to think it was talent and ability combined. There are people who are just amazing at making images and lighting, and there are people who are amazingly good at the software. Then there are sometimes people who can do both. Those who are good at both were considered the best to me. But, now that I manage and direct a team of them, I can say it's more nuanced than that. Really good lighting artists often know it. They can be hard to work with due to ego and sometimes they take a lot of managing because they refuse to work with a team, or to light appropriately to the story or point of the shot/sequence they are working on. A truly good lighting artist has ability and knowhow, but also sees the bigger picture of the animation. They are a storyteller and their lighting works to the greater good of the story instead of showing off their lighting skills individually.

This chapter will go through the lighting setup and execution for each of these three shots.

9

Lighting Walkthroughs

Up until now, this book has been almost strictly theoretical. The discussion has centered on basic lighting terminology and concepts, the structure of a beautiful image, and how to break down the work of others. Now it is time to be light! This chapter will explore three different lighting scenarios and the step-by-step process taken to achieve the final result.

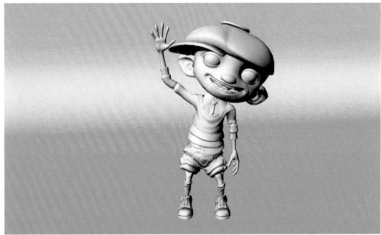

Figure 9.1 *Pio*—beauty lighting. *Pio* is downloadable character courtesy of Boutique23 (www.boutique23.com).

Lighting Scenario One ::
Character Beauty Lighting

One of the most basic lighting scenarios is to ignore any environment and simply make a character look as good and as ideal as possible. This ideal look is generally referred to as "beauty lighting." Beauty lighting consists of lighting a character over a neutral background with light values and colors to complement his or her inherent persona. Often, as in this example, the background is a gray plane that has been curved so it appears as a simple gradient value.

Beauty lighting is commonly done in pre-production when the look of a character is being defined. This part of the schedule is commonly known as the character development phase or the look development phase of a project. Additionally, beauty lighting is also useful when an artist or studio is creating promotional material or print advertisements for the project. For the purposes of this book, beauty lighting will be used to kick off this process of lighting a shot from start to finish.

Pio

For this example, Pio will be the main character. Pio (courtesy of Boutique23) is a twelve-year-old boy from 1930s Chicago and works as a newsie. Pio is an optimistic and outgoing kid and his beauty lighting should represent his overall sunny disposition. Keeping the levels bright and luminous is desired to ensure he is read as a joyful, pleasant kid.

Figure 9.2 The individual lights used during the first breakout of Pio.

Key

The process of lighting normally begins with positioning the key light. In this case, it was decided to position the key light in the upper screen-right side of the image and create Rembrandt Lighting by allowing the light to fall across his face and create strong shaping. When positioning the key light, the focus fell on a few main parts of Pio. The first was his nose. His nose is a spherical shape and the key light was positioned in a way that created strong variation across that round surface. Pio's little nose will not create that triangle of light seen in Rembrandt's work, but the basic principles are still in place.

Another main focus when positioning the key light was on how the shadow cast from his hat was interacting with his eyes. With the focus on keeping him happy, the eyes would ideally not be in complete shadow. But if the key was positioned in a way that both eyes were being illuminated, the light would be too low to the ground and frontal, making the lighting unflattering. The compromise was to position the light where the eye on the screen-right side gets some nice shaping while the screen-left side falls into darkness. It is important to note that the shadow does not slice the eyeball in half, which is distracting when trying to create beauty lighting.

For the color, the decision was made for warm colors simulating a sunny day since that complements his skin tone and generally gives him a healthy glow. To enhance this feeling even further, the shadows on the key light were made very soft. This was accomplished by increasing the light's radius and therefore softening the shadows.

Sky/Fill

For the sky and fill lights, the aim was to create something very broad to illuminate many of the areas not hit by the key light. The difficulty was to accomplish this while not creating a look that was too ambient, flat, and shapeless. In this example, a very broad light was added and positioned above the character. It was angled slightly with an eye toward maintaining visual shaping. In more dramatic, high contrast lighting scenarios this amount of fill would be too much. Given this soft, happy scene, however, this value seemed to meet the aesthetic goals of the shot. The color of the fill was given a cooler tone to keep with the blue sky on a sunny day, but it was definitely desaturated to ensure his skin would stay nice and warm.

Bounce

Once the key, sky, and fill lights were combined, it was noticed that the area under his chin was lacking light. An area light was placed beneath Pio that would help illuminate and fill in this dark section with a little bounce light. The intensity of the light was minimal so as not to compete with the key light's value. This light was also kept on the warmer side to help complement his skin.

Rim

Now there was a lack of variation around the screen-left side of his body and something needed to be done to make his outline distinguishable from the background. A rim light was added to help solve both of these issues. The rim has a lower intensity because it should not be apparent to the audience and it should not compete with the key as the dominant light source. Extra attention was paid to his screen-left hand as the rim light should help accentuate his waving action.

Extra Hand Fill

Once the rim light was added, the front of the waving hand still felt a little under-lit and could have used some additional illumination. Looking back at the render of just the key light in Figure 9.3, it can be seen how the waving hand was being illuminated far less than the brightest part of the face. Normally this would be ideal since the artist wants the attention on the face. But in this particular pose, the audience should also be drawn to the hand and see the character's action. Therefore, a small spotlight was created just to help boost that area and give the hand the illumination necessary to garner attention from the viewer.

Compositing

Now that all the lights were in place, it was time to render the first images and build the comp. As always, the goal was to keep the layering and the comp minimal to avoid an over-complicated workflow. Pio and the background were rendered separately and

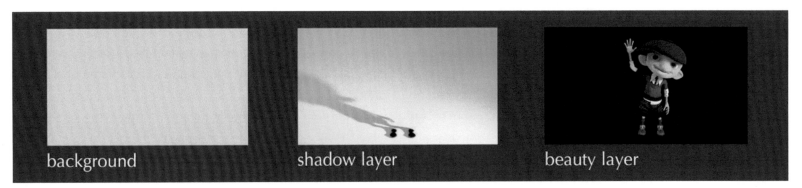

background   shadow layer   beauty layer

Figure 9.3 This initial layer breakout consisted of a background layer, a shadow layer, and a beauty layer.

a shadow pass was created to control the shadow color and quality on the ground. These renders were constructed in the comp and the resulting image can be analyzed to determine the steps needed to improve the image.

Critique :: Round 1

After analyzing the image, there were definitely areas that needed to be addressed for the next iteration. The first was the eyes. The eyes were a bit dead and needed some reflection and a nice ding light. Some extra steps needed to be taken in both the lighting and the compositing in order to resolve the issues.

Another major problem was the shaping on the hat and lower body. Now that everything was analyzed in the composite, they appeared to be frontally lit and in need of a different key light. To solve this issue, a new key light would be created and parented to the hat and lower body geo with a slightly more exaggerated angle in order to create the same successful shaping being seen on the face.

Eyes need some reflection and a ding to give the character life.

This hand is a litle too matte and flat. Some specularity can add some variation. Also, there is a white dot by his thumb that will need to be fixed

The hat and lower body are lacking shaping and could use some relighting to add variation. Also, the legs between his socks and pants feel too glowy and can be taken down in value.

Figure 9.4

key light :: shirt

key light :: lower body

key light :: hat

RGB render 1

RGB render 2

Figure 9.5 Additional render passes created to complete the notes from Critique 1.

Adjustments :: Round 1

The next step was to return to the rendering software to hit the notes. The first note to be addressed was the separate key for the hat, shirt, and lower body. The current key was unlinked to each of these pieces of geometry and additional key lights were added and properly linked to only the necessary geometry. For the hat, the key light was swung around more to the screen-right side and the intensity was increased. The same was true for the lower body, except the amount of rotation was slightly different. The key on the sweater was left in the same position, but the intensity was increased to create a more drastic variation from lightness to dark.

In order to address the issues with the eyes, a couple of new layers needed to be created. The first was an eye reflection pass. The goal of the eye reflection pass was to capture the reflections as they would be seen in the eye. To accomplish this, the outer cornea of the eye was rendered separately and given a material that output a mirrored reflection. The first step was to set all the other geometry in the scene to be visible only in the reflections of the new mirrored eye shader. To add additional reflections of a mock environment, an image was mapped onto a sphere surrounding the character and that sphere is also set to appear only in the reflections. The image chosen for the reflection was also a happy, warm image to match the rest of the scene.

The other render pass that was created was for the eye ding. The goal of the ding layer was to create a single highlight in each eye that would make Pio feel more alive with a twinkle in his eye. The setup was very similar to the reflection pass, but in this case a white, only a circular plane, was added to the scene to appear in the reflections. This white card was scaled and manipulated to give a nice, desirable ding in that ten o'clock position on both eyes. The eye ding was rendered separately from the eye reflections since the intensity and color will often need to be modified in the comp without changing the environmental reflection. The size of the eye ding was on the smaller side and the shape was kept a simple geometric circle so as not to reveal a particular light source being reflected.

RGB mattes were also created to help control each of the areas that have already been identified as problematic. As was discussed earlier in the book, these RGB mattes will help the artist control certain sections of the image in the comp and make minor adjustments that do not require a re-render.

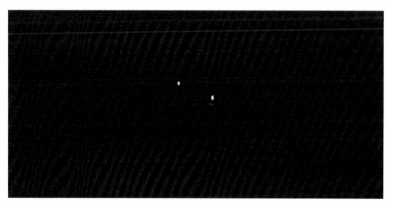

Figure 9.6 Passes for individual eye reflections and an eye ding to help add extra life to the eye.

Critique :: Round 2

The sclera of the eye is a bit too glowy and come down.

There needs to be some contact shadow between the eyeball and the eyelid.

The palm of the waving hand can increase in value slightly.

There is a white line around the hat that will need to be resolved.

The tie is appearing a bit on the dark side and could use some extra intensity to make it pop.

The teeth are a bit too bright and too desaturated.

They need a little bit of warm bounce from the gums back to the teeth.

Figure 9.7

Adjustments :: Round 2

Thanks to the RGB matte passes already created, these notes could be addressed in the comp. A rotoshape and the RGB matte which isolates Pio's waving arm were combined to slightly brighten that area up to the desired level (Figure 9.). Similarly, the teeth were brought down in value slightly and given a little extra warmth with a simple color correction in the comp. The tie was also fixed with a color correction. For the contact shadow on the sclera and the shaping on the shadow side of the face, an ambient occlusion render was created and added to just those regions.

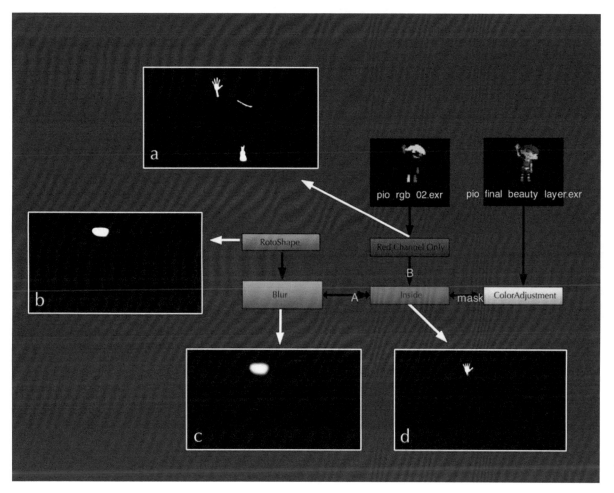

Figure 9.8 The RGB render makes it very easy to isolate certain sections of the image for adjustments. A great example is the note to increase the value of the palm of the waving hand. Since the palm of the hand overlaps the hat, it would be difficult to isolate that area with just a rotoshape. Instead, the RGB matte is utilized by first isolating the red channel (a), then drawing a rotoshape to isolate the desired area (b), then blurring the edge of that rotoshape to avoid hard lines in the color adjustment (c), and merging those two areas together with an "inside" merge operation so the hand is only being used where the change is desired (d). In the end, that image is used as the mask for the color adjustment to increase the value.

Final Image

The final result revealed Pio exemplifying his hero look. His skin and clothing match their hero colors and he has the desired warm, happy glow. Although it took some extra work to get additional shaping on some of his garments, the visual results were worth the effort. In the end, we have an image that can be used to show the ideal look for this character.

Figure 9.9 *Pio*—final image and light positions. *Pio* is downloadable character courtesy of Boutique23 (www.boutique23.com).

Lighting Scenario Two ::
Character and Environment

In most animated projects the character will not be lit alone. Characters normally perform in an environment and a lighting rig must be constructed to work with the entire shot. The character must feel like he or she is both properly illuminated within the scene while also given the proper structure to allow him or her to visually stand off from their surroundings.

In this example, Tre3 is sitting on a set of stairs along a cobblestoned street. He has just been given some news that he must contemplate during this particular evening. This is not an action-packed shot but a calm, thoughtful nature should be expressed in the lighting.

Focusing the Audience's Eye

The biggest challenge this shot presented was creating a rig that would allow the audience to properly focus on Tre3. He was relatively small on camera and not centrally positioned. The lighting should keep the audience's eye on the screen-right side of the image while also giving him proper shaping.

Since there were no lamps or other light sources visibly present in the foreground, the main light sources would exist off camera. This allowed for flexibility in terms of positioning the light source

Figure 9.10 Tre3—alley scene. Tre3 is downloadable character courtesy of Boutique23 (www.boutique23.com). The environment was modeled and shaded by Anuar Figueroa.

Figure 9.11 The key light was created and positioned with the intention of focusing the audience's attention on Tre3 while also creating good shaping on his face and body.

wherever it best aided the aesthetics. The decision was made to have the light source be a lamp on the wall shining from above Tre3. This would create a nice pocket of light that could be used to focus the audience's attention on this section of the image. A couple of locations were tested but ultimately it was determined to have the source coming from the screen-right side, which allowed the door behind Tre3 to remain dark while letting his brighter values come forward. This light position also allowed for shaping similar to Rembrandt Lighting.

Generating Pockets of Light

Another challenge of this shot was expressing the depth and space of the environment. With the key light focusing the audience's attention to one section of the image, secondary lights were added to help define the surroundings. It was important that these secondary sources create pockets of light and dark and not create one flat value. These varying values helped make the scene feel larger and deeper.

If this was a daytime scene, the set would almost be exclusively lit by the natural lighting like the sun and sky and those lights would only be used to create this feeling of depth. This night scene not only had elements of natural light but also allowed the freedom to add artificial lights. Another street lamp was added to the screen-left side and interior lights were added to some of the windows in the background. Their values were carefully dialed in as they needed to be bright enough to give the audience the idea of the set without drawing too much attention away from the focal point.

Creating Shaping in Fill Values

The interior lights of the set not only created brightness on the windows themselves but also spilled light onto the street. This is important because it creates subtle areas of variation that are essential to successful environment lighting. It must always be the focus of the artist to never allow areas to get too flat or evenly lit. Like character lighting, both diffuse and specular values were adjusted to create shaping in these areas.

Adding Softness

The mood of this shot was soft and gentle and some techniques were implemented in order to achieve that look. The first was adding some diffusion by isolating the brighter points in the compositing, blurring them, and then screening them back on top of the original. This created a nice diffusion on the scene that softened some of the harsher edges and gave the overall image a final, more polished look.

Adding depth of field was also implemented to both focus on the main character and also add a

Figure 9.12 After the natural evening sky was added, lights illuminating the windows were created to add depth and variation to the scene.

little extra softness to the image. As previously mentioned, depth of field should be added with care and an understanding of the scale of the scene. But within those boundaries the artist has some wiggle room for dialing in the amount of softness. In this particular case, the decision was made to lean toward heavier blur since that will aid in supplying some softness that will enhance the mood.

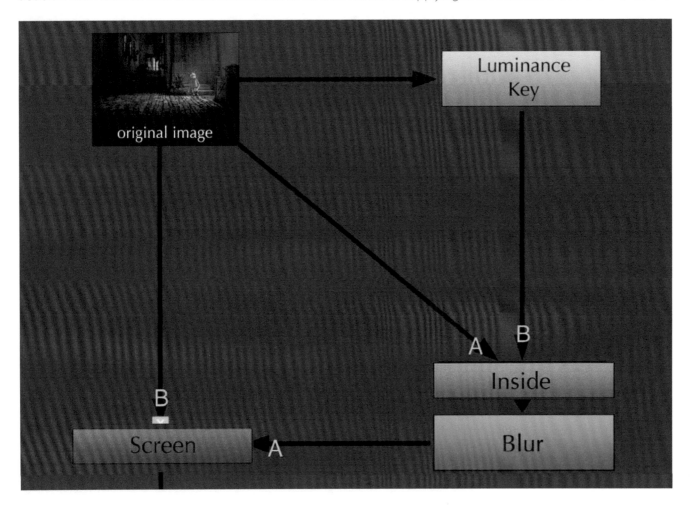

Figure 9.13 Example of using a luminance key to add diffusion to only the highlights of a shot.

Critique :: Round 1

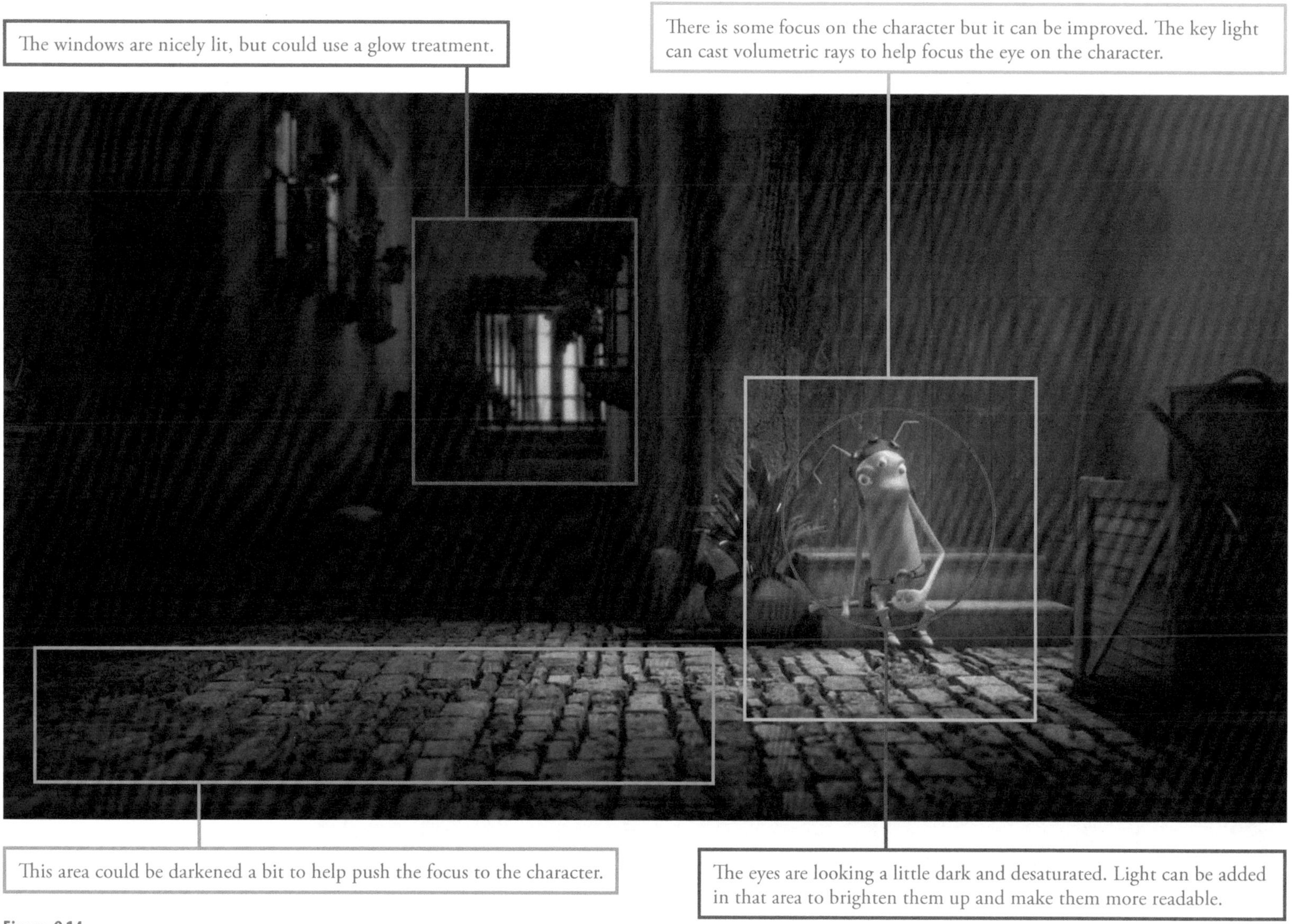

The windows are nicely lit, but could use a glow treatment.

There is some focus on the character but it can be improved. The key light can cast volumetric rays to help focus the eye on the character.

This area could be darkened a bit to help push the focus to the character.

The eyes are looking a little dark and desaturated. Light can be added in that area to brighten them up and make them more readable.

Figure 9.14.

Adjustments :: Round 1

The first note addressed was the eyes. Whenever the eyes are looking too dark or "dirty," the main goal is to add a value and saturation. This was accomplished with a combination of adding lights specifically linked to the eyes and also creating RGB mattes for the eyes to lift the values overall and create a bit of separation between the iris, pupil, and sclera.

To get more focus on the character, a volumetric light was created at the same position as the key light and rendered out as a separate pass. The aesthetic goal of this light was to create a visual path to lead the audience's eye to the character. The edges of the volumetric light were kept soft to keep with the aesthetic. These lights do not need to be harsh lines in order to be effective.

In order to make the rear windows look like glowing light, additional glow and diffusion were created in the comp. Also, the darkening on the screen-left side was accomplished in the composite by drawing a soft rotoshape around that area and darkening the gamma and multiplying the overall value down.

Figure 9.15 A volumetric light was created at the same location as the key light to add some more mood and to serve as a leading line for the viewer's attention.

Critique :: Round 2

The plant in front of the window should appear more translucent with so much light behind it. The shader will need to be adjusted.

Figure 9.16

The wall facing the camera could be darker. This will help push the viewer's eye back to the right side of the screen and allow more distiction between the three screen-lit walls.

The key light has some volumetric light to appear stronger and now the bounce light could be increased to help rebalance his lighting. Also, the amount of diffusion on Tre3 is a bit strong.

Adjustments :: Round 2

The value of the key light plus the quality of the surface area beneath the character equals the resulting bounce light. Therefore, since we added this volumetric light, the image appeared to have more key value and the area of Tre3's body normally filled in by the bounce looked weak. The bounce light was increased by about 25 percent in order to accommodate.

The walls on the screen-left side of the frame were starting to merge together in value. The wall going down the side alley was also appearing to be a bit flat and could use more variation. In order to keep the attention on the screen-right side, the decision was made to darken the overall value of that wall but also to give it a subtle variation in color in order to give it more visual shaping.

The last modification was altering the material value of the far background leaves close to the window. In nature, these leaves have a translucent value that allows light to pass through them. By default, the shader on the leaves did not have that quality since it was assumed they would be so far away from camera to justify that added calculation time. Only after the lighting was added was it apparent that this quality was missing. This is often the case and one of the many reasons why lighting and shaders work so closely together. The modification was made and the leaves now have a more natural translucent quality.

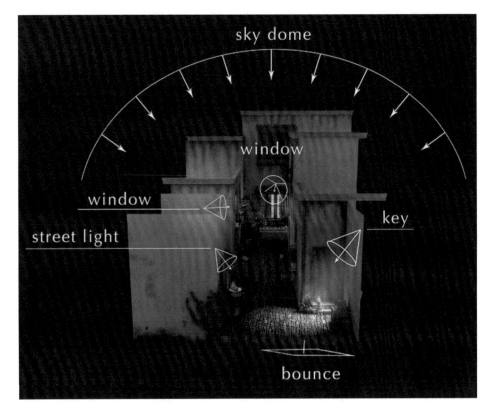

Figure 9.17 Tre3—alley scene. Light positions for the final image.

Final Image

Figure 9.18

Figure 9.19 Party time!!!

Lighting Scenario Three :: Multiple Characters

There are often lighting situations that require an atypical approach. They do not fall into the normal lighting scenarios and require some extra research and vision in order to make them successful. For this example, the entire light bulb family is going dancing. It is either a wedding or some other family event where the whole family is celebrating together. Everyone is invited from grandfather to granddaughter and even the puppy. It is a jovial, cheerful engagement and the lighting, colors, and overall feeling must convey that emotion.

To begin a unique lighting situation like this it was essential to gather reference and determine a direction of the final look before proceeding. Research was done and the film *Saturday Night Fever* was chosen as a very general basis for several reasons. Obviously, this film has an iconic look that is whimsical, fun, and playful. The goal was to create a unique look by building this lighting design. The second reason this reference was chosen was the darkness in the areas around the main characters. The CG set in this example is extremely minimal with only the characters, dance floor, and a couple of simple set pieces. In these situations it is up to the lighter to craft a scene that allows the audience to mentally extend that space and believe the environment is more elaborate than it actually is.

The Floor

The first step in tackling the obstacle of lighting this scene was the glowing dance floor. When approaching a challenge like this it was important to try and conceptualize how that structure was constructed. Analyzing the reference made it appear as though there was a top, transparent glass dance floor with the colored tiles below. The colored tiles appeared to have a light source in the center that decreased in intensity as it reached the edge of each square.

It was important to construct the geometry in a similar method to get the same effect. A plane was laid as the top layer and given a slightly frosted glass material. Individual planes were placed below this glass floor and given a glowing material that had a ramp controlling the intensity from the center outward. These squares were given colors and arranged in a geometric pattern that was similar to the reference.

Figure 9.20 *Saturday Night Fever*—© mptvimages.com.

Figure 9.21 Each of the illuminating floor tiles was given a ramped texture to make it appear like there was a glowing bulb beneath the floor.

The Disco Ball

The disco ball was intriguing on a few levels. The mirrored surface gathered much of its illumination from reflecting the light of brighter objects around it. Disco balls also create a unique pattern of refracted light hitting the surrounding environment. Since the ball was made up of individual, square mirrors, the refracted light appeared to be many individual specks of light following the rotation of the ball. Last, disco balls always seem to have a magical aura surrounding them. In many of the reference images found, disco balls are given an extra glow or lens flare to make them appear more beautiful.

A few elements were needed to be placed in order to get the disco ball working successfully. The first was getting the lighting and shaping on the object itself working. The next step was making sure the disco ball had enough elements to reflect to be properly illuminated in the space. This can be done by constructing an entire set and lighting it even if the objects are off camera. In this particular case, however, the decision was made to instead add a reflection map to the scene to give the disco ball something to reflect, since this would be much more efficient during the rendering phase. This was done by placing a sphere around the disco ball that only appears in the reflection of the object. The sphere's visibility was turned off along with its ability to cast or receive shadows. Then an image mimicking the surrounding set was mapped to that sphere and the reflection was set.

A unique light rig was constructed in order to achieve the sparkling lights surrounding the disco ball. This rig consisted of six spotlights all placed at the center of the disco ball and projecting

Figure 9.22 The disco ball sprays hundreds of little dots of light around the room. Our gobo map was created to do the same thing with colors that match the lights used.

light in each direction around the room. The disco ball's visibility was turned off to avoid it casting shadows. These lights were given gobo maps that have the same square shape as the individual pieces of the mirrored ball. Finally, the light rig was parented to the disco ball itself to ensure it would properly rotate when the disco ball was animated.

The Volumetric Lights

Another element that was observed in the reference was strong volumetric lights focused on the dance floor. These did a great job of directing the viewer's eye while also masking off areas of the background that are bare and empty. The lights were also a beautiful streak of color that added playfulness to the scene.

Character Lighting

The first step was to establish an overall value for the characters since they all needed to be visible and readable over the dark background. They were each given enough light to pop out from the dark surroundings, but not enough to feel out of place. The characters on the dance floor were the main focus so their illumination was even a touch brighter than those characters standing off to the side.

As far as the specifics of light direction, the focus once again went to the reference image to begin the process. How much light was shining on them from the glowing floor? How were the characters being illuminated by the surrounding overhead spotlights? How saturated should the light color get? The reference showed an overall red fill value that illuminated the main characters. That

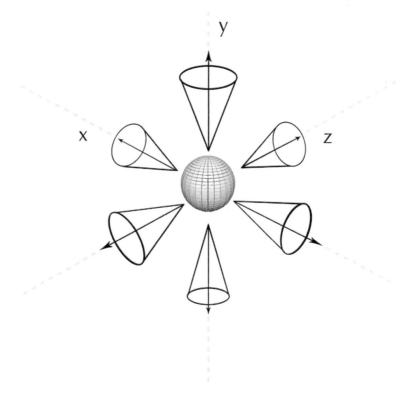

Figure 9.23 The light emitting from the disco ball is actually six different spotlights emitting light in all directions.

fill value is also accompanied by several colorful rim lights that not only integrated the characters into the space but also made them look more beautiful. This image was made with the same structure in mind with slight modifications to match the desired color palette.

Critique :: Round 1

The light could appear brighter since the brightest point is a clamped gray valve.

The disco ball was too dark and could use some more light and reflections.

The gobo map is too large and creating shapes that are too big in the background.

The dance floor colors are too saturated and did not feel glowy enough. The characters also do not feel like they were influenced by that light.

The character lighting is weak. More shaping and color should be contributed by the rim lights. The character's materials are not holding up under the lighting scenario. There are more value differences that are not being detected under the colored lights. Edits will need to be made in order to create better variation. Also, the current reflections in the character's bulb are not aesthetically appealing.

The background is getting pure black and needs to have some value in order to be believable.

Figure 9.24

Adjustments :: Round 1

When faced with a long list of notes, some prefer to attack the easiest notes first to gain momentum before approaching the more difficult challenges. In this case, increasing the intensity of the volumetric lights was easy. After that, the color of the dance floor was desaturated and the incandescent intensity was increased to create more of a glow. Then the size of the gobo map was decreased and tiled to create smaller points of light around the room.

From there it was on to the disco ball. At first more lights were created to light the disco ball but that was only adding specular values to the mirrored surface. In order to make the ball appear brighter, the reflection map was initially increased but it was difficult to determine the proper value. Instead, a separate reflection pass for the sphere was created so the exact brightness could be controlled in the comp. An RGB specular pass was also created to add some highlights to the ball.

To add some additional value to the background, a magenta light fog was added to the room. There is a little of this haze present in the reference image and just adding that bit of value can make a very dark space feel more realistic.

For the characters, the materials needed to be adjusted before anything else could be done. The lighter and darker components of their clothing were exaggerated in order for the audience to see the difference. This is a common tweak when working in bizarre lighting scenarios because material values can appear very different depending on their surroundings.

The reflection on the bulbs also needed to be modified. The layout of the space was creating reflections that were unappealing and confusing. To improve this the reflective properties of the bulbs were turned off in the character render and a separate bulb reflection pass was created to replace it. In that layer the surrounding geometry's main visibility was turned off so it would only appear in the reflections and refractions. Then all the surrounding geometry was slightly adjusted so the reflections were still believable but more aesthetically appealing.

Critique :: Round 2

The volumetric lights are nice, but some additional elements can be added to make them feel special.

The disco ball could also use something more to make it feel magical. Also it is a little neutral for the space and could use more influence from the magenta surrounding color.

After viewing the reference again, the spots are actually larger the further away they get from the disco ball. Also, the overall density of the disco spots can be increased.

The dance floor feels a little flat and could use something extra to make it look like it is glowing.

The character's filaments should be turned on to give them a bit more life. Although these characters don't have eyes, their filaments work as a focal point and are similar to their eye dings. There are some dark values on the characters that could be lifted.

A little more vignetting could be added to the bottom two corners of the frame to keep the audience's attention on the characters.

Figure 9.25

Adjustments :: Round 2

To address the filament note, two separate elements needed to be in place. The first was the glowing filament itself and the second was that light's influence on its surroundings. The glow was first attempted in the render, but after some testing it was determined that the glow value could be more easily controlled in the comp. A matte layer was created that allowed those filaments to be isolated in the comp and controlled accordingly.

The bulb's influence on the surrounding elements was achieved by placing a point light at each position where there was a filament. That point light was given a decay rate so it would only influence the area directly around it. This was also rendered as a separate pass so the filament color and the resulting light could match.

Some compositing techniques were utilized to allow the disco ball and volumetric lights to feel more magical. Adding a bit of added diffusion or light glow to these regions was the first step. Both the specular highlights of the disco ball and the bulbs of these volumetric lights were extremely bright compared with the rest of the scene so it was believable that they would create this softness. The next step that went along with this brightness was to add a small amount of lens flare. These two elements should be applied with a gentle hand to avoid looking hokey, but if just the right balance is met they can provide the image with a little extra magic.

Figure 9.26 Party time — light positions for final image.

The final steps included lifting the blacks beneath a few of the characters by increasing the bounce value, increasing the value of the dance floor lights to make them look like they are glowing, adding a little darkening in the two bottom corners of the frame to create a little more vignetting, and color correcting the disco ball slightly to have a bit more of the magenta color of the room.

Final Image

Figure 9.27

Final Thoughts

If there is any overarching concept to take away from this chapter it would be that no two lighting scenarios are the same. There is no single approach to lighting that will work in every instance. Every scenario will present its own set of challenges that must be solved in a variety of ways. These walkthroughs are not the only solution but simply one way to approach these situations. The key is to remember the core fundamentals of lighting and strive to reach those in every shot: create shaping, direct the viewer's eye, and tell the story.

Interview
with Yann Mabille

Creative Director/Partner :: Interstate.

Q. What is your current job/role at your company?
A. My current role is Creative Director/Partner at Interstate. Previously, I was a Director at Mill+.

Q. What inspired you to work in this industry?
A. There were many factors that inspired me to work in this industry. Back when I started in 1995, it felt like you were part of a team of pioneers. We were all exploring a new medium which allowed us not only to create images never seen before, but also to bring whole worlds to life through animation and direct digital translation of traditional cinema techniques. The technological aspect of this industry also made a huge impression on me. The technology was just fascinating to me as an artist as nothing then was taken for granted and it all really seemed like mysterious science. It really was a relief that 3D imagery was actually made, even back then, by artists and not computer gurus. I was lucky to have been mentored by a team of incredibly talented people. I started as a 3D artist in France. Back then 3D imagery was something very special that really seemed to come out of the mind of mysterious computer wizards. I was lucky to live in a city that was home to one of the best 3D companies in France which was called Gribouille and had won technical prizes at the Imagina festival. They had a Cyberscan which was one of the first in Europe and that allowed the scanning of human faces. The whole company was equipped with Silicon Graphics machines running IRIX and Softimage 2.6. To put things in context, not a single person in the company had an email when I started as an intern. It just was not widespread then. I interrupted my graphic art studies to become a full-time employee at Gribouille.

Right now my work is different in the way that I focus less on detail and more on the conceptual aspect of the project. I do not create any CGI any more but I am able to creatively guide teams and make sure we all create high quality visuals.

Q. What non-CG artwork inspires you?

A. I enjoy traditional illustration a lot. Children's books are incredibly creative and the techniques are very diverse. Comics have always been a huge source of inspiration for me, be it through the storytelling aspect or technique. I was greatly inspired by Juan Giménez with the work he did for the "Caste des Méta-Barons," also by Philippe Caza who I was incredibly lucky to work with. His intricate science fiction book covers let your imagination run wild. Of course, the incredibly influential Moebius and Philippe Druillet who created *Heavy Metal* magazine. I was also lucky to have worked with Druillet at Gribouille to make a pilot for *Excalibur*. Comics in France are considered as the ninth art and have been extremely influential and are still today for me. I also like land art a lot. Andy Goldsworthy is a master. His work is incredibly modest but very powerful and at the same time fragile. Since I have been living in the US, I have been more attentive to French cinema and as a result American independent cinema, which I am a big fan of. I also admire Théo Jansen, who creates admirable kinetic sculptures that look like they could be other animal beings.

Q. Can you tell us a little bit of how lighting plays a role when working on a job?

A. Be it a fully CG job or a hyper-realistic CG element composited in a live action plate, lighting is obviously key. Without good quality lighting, the job simply will not look good. Lighting sets the mood of a movie or a commercial, it allows the design and textures of characters and assets to come to life and express their specific beauty. Lighting is the conduit for expression. Without light, you would not see. With great lighting, everything becomes beautiful in its own right.

Q. How important is lighting to the process when you are integrating a CG element in a live action plate as opposed to working on a fully animated shot?

A. In a realistic job, the role of lighting is to solely replicate the lighting setup on set to achieve maximum realism for a good integration. In this context, the approach is a bit more technical as the artist either has to use data gathered on set to light his scene, or replicate the lighting on set using his artistic abilities, or both. Well, that's in theory; sometimes the artist has to add a little extra to make the CG asset perfectly integrated. Overall, the live action is what drives the artist's choices. In a fully CGI project, the lighting approach is more free as it is not limited to just recreating the setup of the live action plate. As a result, lighting can be more expressive in projects like this. Every scene that composes a shot becomes a mini set into which physical lighting rules can be broken. Unlike a live action set, every component here can be controlled, which is a great canvas for an artist.

Q. What kind of assets do you like to provide for the lighters when shooting on set? For example, do you always provide reference of the lighting rig/environment, create HDRI images …?

A. It is now a standard to capture HDRI data on set. It is recommended but obviously not essential. It allows a faster turnaround time and more precise lighting and reflections. However, an artist should be able to go beyond the HDRI data or even not use it at all. In the end, it's all about the artist's eye and how a specific lighting setup can be recreated to achieve seamless integration. Lighting is never plug and play. There is always a little something to improve or a way to cheat perception to make CG work better within the live action plate. There is no set recipe to create a realistic render. Every situation is different, there are very different methods and approaches. In the end, what is important is that the artist has a good sense of observation and analysis.

Q. In commercial work, what is the standard amount of time a lighting artist has to work on a shot? Is their role strictly lighting or do they take on other responsibilities like shaders and compositing?

A. In commercial work a lighter not only sets up the lighting in the 3D scene, but also sets up shaders and digs into compositing to make sure his renders fit within the live action. The shaders are somewhat dependent on lighting and vice versa, so it makes sense for the artist to refine both at the same time. Again, this is in the commercial world. Also, the artist needs to see further down the pipeline, hence why, in general, he does pre comps to see how big the range is in 2D to achieve the right integration. The bigger the range, the more off the asset is and the more it will need 2D work. With a smaller range, the tweaks in 2D will be minimal, which means the 3D render is good.

Q. If you could tell yourself one piece of advice when you were first starting out in this industry, what would it be?

A. The generic answer is to follow your passion, of course. I realized quite a lot of people did not have a true passion for the medium, which can only bring you to a certain level. Beyond this, a lot of people do think that CGI is just knowing the tools. They think that the software alone will allow them to make great visuals. The computer is going to "sort it out" for them. By pressing the right button, using the right renderer, they will be great artists. Some schools are all about promoting the latest software, technique, etc.. Forget all this and trust your eye and your instinct. In the end, an artist is someone who is sensitive to certain things in life that mostly everyone else will not perceive. Use your own perception, tap into it and exploit it through the CGI medium.

Q. Where do you think the future of lighting is headed?

A. I would say real time lighting. Real time engines are getting closer to using algorithms used by non real time renderers. The overall building process is similar, which is great for the artists. A 3D artist who uses the Unreal Engine 4 editor will feel familiar with Maya and vice versa. Obviously they are different software and will require adaptation time but the approaches from both are merging. The real time approach is less forgiving in the preparation of assets right now but a lot more flexible once you actually start lighting. Eventually, I think a 3D artist will be using virtual headsets to light scenes in real time.

Q. What's the one spot or shot you are most proud to have worked on?

A. I am proud of some of the work I did when I first started and some very recent work. By today's standards the old work, which was mostly game cinematics, is not comparable to what is done today and the software has evolved dramatically. At that time, modeling was literally creating vertices one by one, then adding edges one by one to make polygons. Things were different; it was labor intensive but incredibly rewarding. I was proud of the work because at the time it was some of the best. I am thinking of long nights rendering a pilot for the *Dungeon Keeper 2* cinematics which involved the "Reaper" squashing chickens. What a lot of fun that was! Recently, I am proud of some work I directed: one is a promo for the series *Penny Dreadful* on Showtime which is called "Just Like You" and the other is a Hallmark commercial I also directed about two years ago which is called "Mother Bird" and features fully CG birds.

Q. In your opinion, what makes a good lighting artist?

A. To recreate a world you don't have to understand how the real world is built. You don't really have to know the science behind lighting to recreate good lighting. All you need to do is to be attentive to the world around you. You need to trust your sense of observation and analyze what you see so that it makes sense to you. You have to constantly be on the lookout to see things that other people bypass. You have to observe the world from an artist's perspective, which is constantly trying to absorb specific details about the environment around you. Also, what do you feel like when you are present in a specific situation? Do you feel more melancholic on a stormy day? Do you feel more relaxed on a rainy day? These are different moods that do affect you as an artist and that once digested will help you create similar moods in CG. You have to let yourself be sensitive and somewhat understand what affects you and absorb as much as you can around you. Artists are sensitive beings because they are sensitive to their surroundings.

10

Master Lighting

Rarely are shots lit in isolation. Shots are often part of a larger project and must be treated as just one small piece of a much larger puzzle. Certain factors must be taken into consideration when lighting a shot that is destined to be a part of a film, television show, commercial, or animated short. What is the purpose of the shot? Is the key coming from the same direction in every shot? Does the character's color match from shot to shot? Regardless of whether this is being applied to a thirty-second commercial or a ninety-minute feature, master lighting is a fundamental process that can benefit any project.

This chapter will cover the fundamentals of master lighting and how to transform multiple shots from concept designs to final images.

Lighting Pre-production

Organizing Sequences

Every studio and pipeline functions differently but there are some core workflows many studios use when handling these types of projects. The first step is to package shots together into sequences. These sequences consist of a series of sequential shots normally unified by time of day and/or location. For a commercial project or animated short there may be just one or two sequences. Entire films are made up of many sequences that tell small narratives and make up the overall story arc.

Story Boards

A common method for starting a sequence is to create traditional storyboards. Storyboards are illustrations or drawings designed to represent the shots that will make up a project. In many ways they are like a comic book as they give a panel-by-panel account of the action. Storyboards are used as a pre-visualization to help envision the story and how it will unfold on screen.

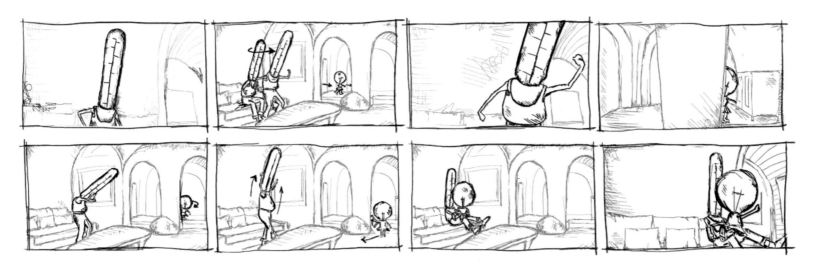

Figure 10.1 Sequence storyboard.

Contact Sheets

Artists take the storyboards and roughly translate that initial vision into the computer. The storyboard frames are replaced with a contact sheet showing a visual representation of a single frame from each shot. This contact sheet is important because it gives artists a visual look at how all the shots in the sequence fit together. A contact sheet is particularly beneficial where there are multiple artists on a single project. As the shots are lit, artists update the contact sheet with lit frames so everyone is aware of any changes and can adjust their own shots accordingly. This allows them the ability to work together to ensure the sequence maintains a consistent look and visually ties together.

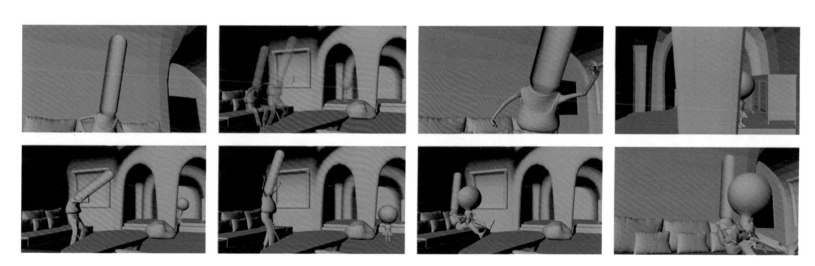

Figure 10.2 Contact sheet.

Look Development and Master Lighting

Not all lighters are given the opportunity to complete master lighting. This is normally given to the most experienced artists and those who are trusted with the responsibility for making aesthetic decisions for the good of the project. Studios will often create Master Lighter or Lighting Lead job titles to distinguish those who complete this task.

The main artistic goal of master lighting is to define the look of the sequence through the process of look development. This is the time when the lighting artist can experiment with different methods to help determine the best approach possible to lighting the sequence with aesthetic beauty and render efficiency. Sometimes there are color keys given to the artist that can provide a general idea of what the director has in mind for the look and colors. Other times there are character style sheets that show all the reference images associated with a particular character or prop piece. If either of these is present, the lighter strives to match that initial design and deliver the director his or her vision.

Even the largest animated features, color keys and style sheets are certainly not a given on any project. There are instances in which there is no time to create a visual color key due to a short production schedule or last-minute changes. In these situations, the lighting artist must translate what he or she is verbally told about the sequence into visual elements. The direction will be something along the lines of "Make it look like morning, but kind of an eerie, mysterious morning." Or, "I really liked the look of this one particular painting. Try and give this sequence the same feeling." It is then the master lighter's responsibility to meet the supervisor's expectations.

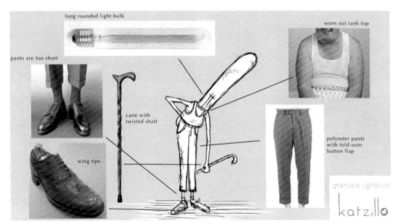
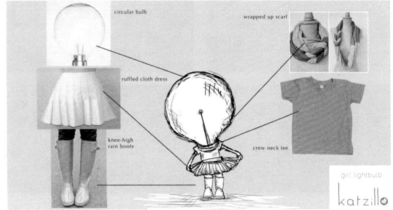

Figure 10.3 Character style sheets.

During look development, there are a multitude of questions that need to be answered about the sequence lighting including large questions like:

- What time of day is it?
- Where is the sun positioned?
- Which man-made lights are on and what is the quality of light they produce? Are they flickering or static?
- How much do the surrounding lights contribute to the character's fill value?

There are also smaller, more detailed looks that need to be established during the course of master lighting.

- Are the leaves on the trees more of a cool green or a yellow, warmer green?
- How saturated is the sky color?
- How bright are the scleras of the eyes?
- At what speed does the candlelight flicker?
- How much caustic bounce reflects off the water onto the environment?
- How saturated and how dense is the aerial perspective?

If a color key is provided, many of these questions can be answered by referencing a color key before going into your computer to light.

Figure 10.4 These color keys were created by rendering the 3D file with an ambient light and digitally painting over the frame with the desired color and luminance. This is an excellent timesaving method for creating a color key.

From analyzing these color keys, one can come to the following conclusions even before opening the scene to light:

- This is either a night scene or taking place in a room without access to outdoor lighting.
- The main light sources include a cool light coming from a TV and the hallway light which is warmer in tone.
- The position of the TV can be determined by looking at the position of the shadow it casts from the character onto the environment..
- The TV will be flickering so that must be taken into account when creating the lighting rig.
- Since the grandfather begins these shots very upset and ends very happy, the color of his filament will change from cool to warm to reflect this emotion. This ability to transform must also be accounted for in the light rig.

Picking Master Shots

Individual master shots from each sequence are selected in order to begin the master lighting process. Master shots are a handful of shots that can be used to represent the overall look of the entire sequence. Each main character and all major environmental elements that exist in the sequence should appear in at least one master shot. This will allow a master look to be determined for those elements and all subsequent shots will match that design.

There is no set number of master shots that must exist for a certain sequence. Simple sequences can have as few as one or two, while complex sequences can have many more. The key is to be efficient with the selections to ensure that the look for the sequence can be determined with as few shots as possible.

Looking at the sequence on the next page, the master lighter chose the following master shots. These master shots were chosen to group similar camera angles and actions together. In this case, the master shots were chosen in this way:

- Shots 212_001 and 212_003 are similar camera angles and contain the same character.
- Shots 212_002, 212_004, 212_005 focus on the same areas of the sequence with the same lighting mood.
- Shots 212_008, 212_007, and 212_006 have the same camera as 212_002 and 212_004 but the lighting mood is different. As can be seen from the color key in the above section (Figure 10.5), it is in the later part of the sequence where Grandpa's mood transforms so it is acceptable to group these shots with their own master.

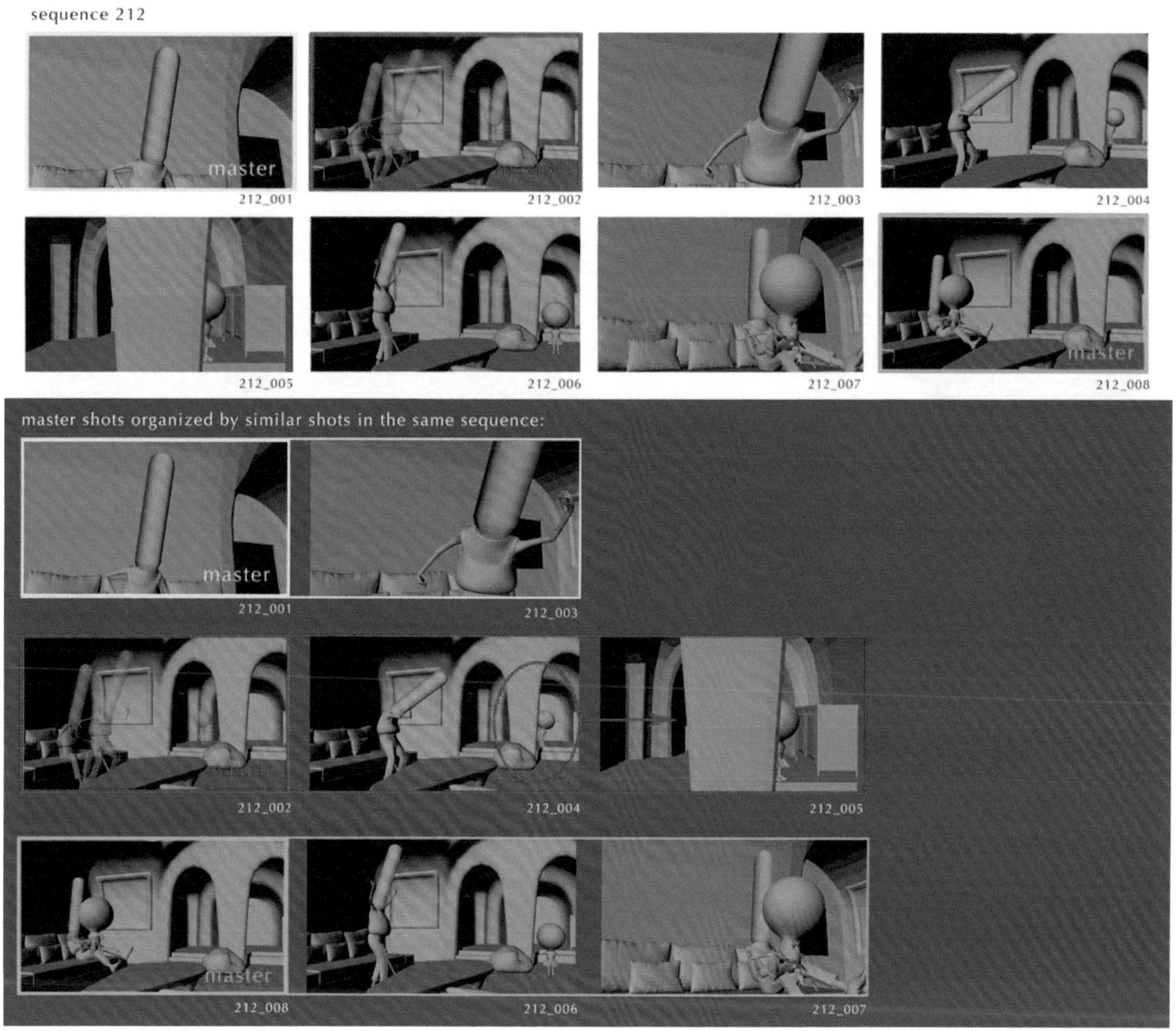

sequence 212

master shots organized by similar shots in the same sequence:

Figure 10.5 Master shots are chosen and bundled with shots containing similar objects, camera angles, and actions.

Creating a Clean Rig

The other element that must be taken into consideration during the master lighting process is organization and structure. The master lighting rig will be propagated to many shots and should contain good naming conventions and a predictable, structural order. The lights should be properly named and set up with the intention of being imported into other shots and easily understood by all artists.

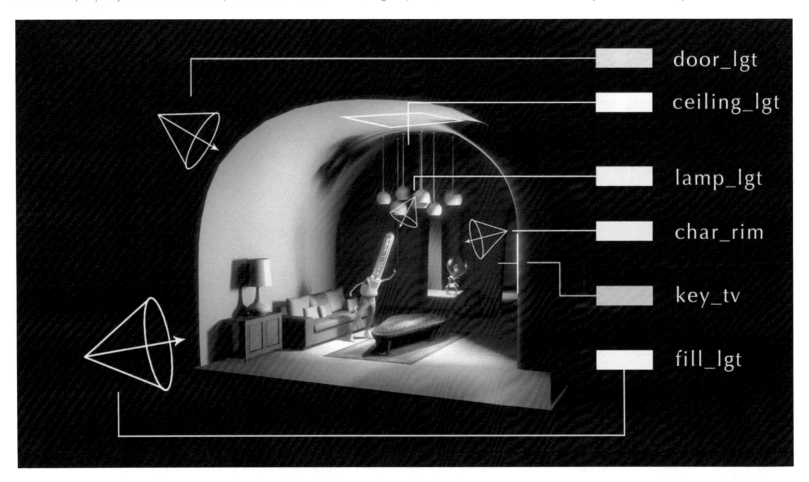

Figure 10.6 A diagram of the master lighting rig including the position of each light and its color.

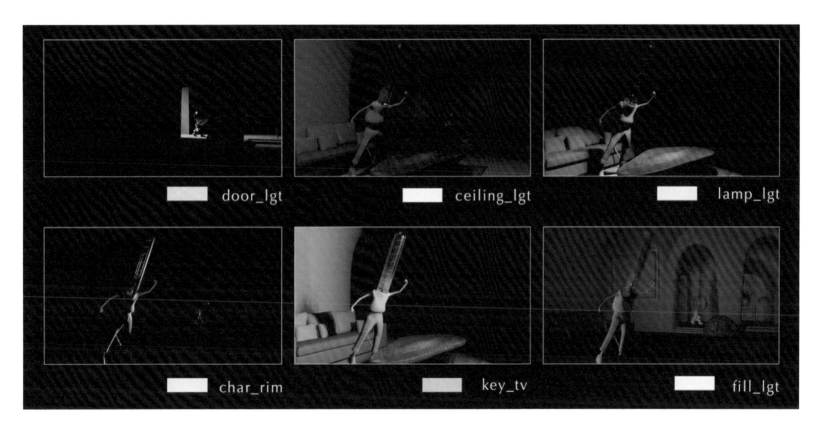

Figure 10.7 Renders of each individual light isolated showing its contribution to the final look.

Naming Conventions

In the previous section, it was mentioned that the lights should be properly named. This means creating a naming convention and sticking to it throughout the project. The key to a good naming convention is one that is consistent and predictable. The specifics of the names do not matter as much as that all artists involved know exactly what to expect and that it remains the same from shot to shot and sequence to sequence. Crucial time would be wasted if each artist needed to learn a whole new system every time a shot was lit. Creating and implementing a proper naming structure may take an extra few minutes during setup, but the time savings in the long run could be monumental.

There is no universal, standard system for naming lights but there are some descriptive terms that should be in most light rig naming conventions. These include the type of light (key, fill, rim, etc.), the position of the light (screen-right, from_above, etc.), and whether the light is linked to any specific character or geometry plus any other descriptive value. The descriptors should be written in the same order since that could make it easier to write a script later to manipulate all the lights named "key" or all the lights associated with a specific character.

Make it Clean

When designing the light rig, it is of the utmost importance to try and keep it as clean and as simple as possible. Remember, whether an artist is working alone or with others, any sloppy or inefficient setups in the master rig will make for a messy workflow. There are a few pitfalls with creating master lighting that should be avoided.

The first is to eliminate anything within the rig that is inefficient and can unnecessarily increase render times. Any lights that are casting soft shadows that are not necessary will drastically increase render times and should be modified. Lights that have decay turned on when it is not causing a visual impact should be modified. Do what is needed to ensure that each render calculation is necessary for the final look of the render.

This can mean going through the geometry and materials as well. Is there a bunch of objects off camera that do not cast shadows onto the scene and that can be removed from the 3D file? Is there a bookcase in the far background where each book has a 4K texture map? Could those files be reduced with no visual consequence? Although these are not necessarily part of the light rig, these types of changes will make the lighting artist's life much better come render time.

The second pitfall is avoiding any animated values or other shot-specific tweaks in the master lights. Obviously each rig will need to be adjusted for the given shot, but things like animating the intensity or position of the light should be avoided in the master rig as they can easily get copied over and cause problems in all other shots. If those types of tweaks are necessary, make sure to create a separate file with all those adjustments removed as the starting point for the other shots.

The third pitfall is not properly documenting and explaining the light rig so that all involved can be on the same page. The artists should know the inspiration behind the look and some of the visual cues of the particular sequence. It is great if the master light rig has all these specialty lights that make the master shot look wonderful, but if that information is not properly communicated to the rest of the team that beauty will be lost in subsequent shots. Verbally communicating this is great, but written documentation is even better. By creating a written record of the information, the artists can use that as a reference point when working on their own shots.

Keep Layers to a Minimum

Just as it is a goal to keep the master lighting rig as simple as possible, it is also wise to always strive for a simple solution in regard to render layers. For a sequence with several artists, adding unnecessary render layers can over-complicate the pipeline and lead to slower and less consistent results. The more variables that exist in the master rig, the more are the chances of the shots being inconsistent with one another.

Specific render layers such as specular passes or reflection passes are often broken out due to necessity, speed, and control for a particular shot. It is important to note that those layers should not be created as the default every time. Simpler rigs, fewer render layers, faster render times, and overall organization and communication equal happier shot lighters!

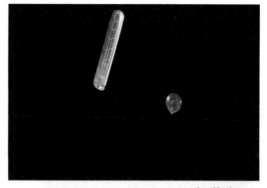

bulb layer

body layer

Figure 10.8 Render layers used.

set layer

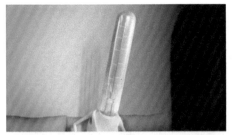

character without glow

matte for glow

glow done in post

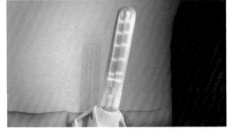

character with glow

Comp

Good compositing skills go hand in hand with good lighting. When master lighting, the artist should isolate what elements can be more easily done in the comp, rather than in lighting. In this instance, the lighter chose to create the "glow" effect from the light bulb in postproduction. This is because it gives the artists greater control when the light needs to animate not only in intensity but also in color.

Master Lighting APPROVED! Making Shots Match

Once all of these questions have been answered and the final look of the master shots has been established, it is time to coordinate the remainder of the sequence. As the first phase of this process is termed "master lighting," the second phase is termed "shot lighting." The main goal of shot lighting is for each shot to be aesthetically sound while matching the approved look determined by the master shots so the entire sequence flows smoothly.

Shot lighting begins by taking the master light rig and placing it in all the remaining shots in the sequence. Often an initial render is done and the first step is for the artist to analyze how well the shot is matching the master. Is the key light coming from the proper angle given the direction the character is looking on the set? Do the characters have the same skin tone or spec level? What about the background: do the color and hue of the leaves match from one shot to the next? If anything is out of line, it is the lighter's responsibility to match everything up. The master light rig will almost always need to be adjusted to alleviate shot-specific problems and to ensure that everything is matching up.

Figure 10.9 A breakdown of the layers used to create the filament glow effect.

Figure 10.10 Approved master lighting shots.

A/B comparison:

slide viewer comparison:

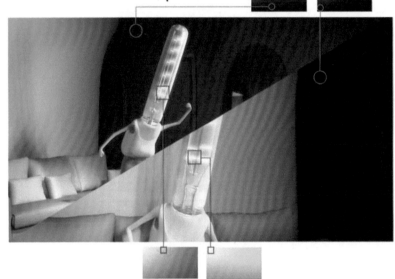

corrected:

 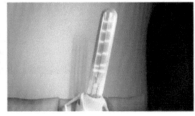

Viewing Tricks for Analyzing Differences in Shots

There are tricks to helping an artist compare frames to ensure shots are matching. The artist is specifically looking for elements like color quality (hue/saturation), light intensity, contrast levels, black points and white points (the value of the lightest and darkest pixels in the frame). Generally speaking, an artist can better judge the values of a shot when visually comparing between frames instead of working from memory.

One method is to quickly switch back and forth between a single frame of two shots to compare values. The artist can stare at the values and do this rapid comparison multiple times to make any variations stand out. Many image editors and compositing software packages give the user the ability to compare frames this way.

Another method involves aligning similar objects from different shots side by side so their differences will become apparent. Most compositing packages have a viewing option that will allow the artist to do it through the viewer, but it can easily be set up with a merge function as well.

Figure 10.11 By viewing two frames from different shots side by side the artist can more easily match colors and values.

Shot Continuity

Shot continuity must be analyzed when going through a sequence. This process ensures that the lighting flows along seamlessly from shot to shot. If a character runs into the shadows in one shot, they should also be starting in shadow in the next shot. It must remain one continuous visual timeline in order for the audience to maintain believability. It is only by repeatedly looping the shots and checking the updated contact sheet that the artist can get the full grasp of the final product.

Final Thoughts

A question often asked by those entering the industry is how much influence a lighter has over the final look of the shot. While it is true that a lighter does have control over individual shots, there will never be a greater time than master lighting to influence aesthetics. This is the time when the big decisions are made and the artist has the ability to put his or her stamp on the project.

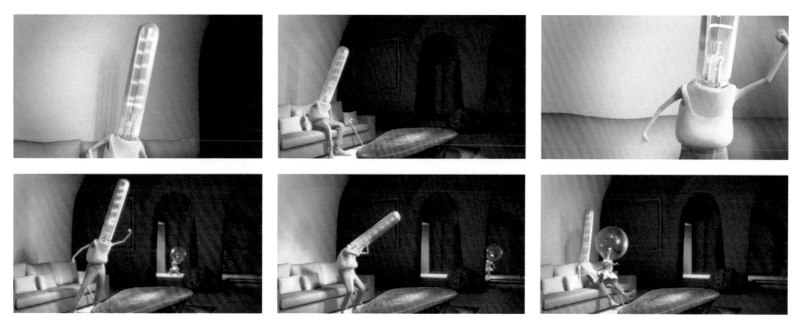

Figure 10.12 Final stills from multiple shots in this sequence.

Interview
with Eldar Cholich

Lead Lighting Artist :: Blue Sky Studios.

Q. What is your current job/role at your company?

A. I am a Lead Lighting Artist at Blue Sky Studios. My responsibilities in this role can be categorized in two main parts. On one hand, at the start of lighting my job is to collaborate with the lighting supervisor, art director and director to define the general look and feel of the sequence through the process of master lighting. On the other side, once we get the buyoff from the director on the master shots, I switch gears into a more supporting role and guide a team of lighting artists through the process of shot lighting of that sequence, advising them on any problems that they might encounter as they take their shots from initial breakouts through approval. There are also some overarching administrative and technical aspects to my role, such as making shot assignment packets, troubleshooting issues, and reporting inventory problems to other departments, and generally way too much email correspondence, but I don't usually like to mention those, since they are not as fun.

Q. What inspired you to become an artist on CG films?

A. I've always been fascinated by movies. Ever since I was a child, I was inspired by stories that moved me. I think this is something that we all share and that is unique to us as a species. Since the cavemen days, we have been exploring new and more exciting ways to tell our stories. The invention of moving pictures is a natural extension of this urge. We can create entire worlds of limitless complexity, and with CG those worlds can take realistic shape that we could only dream of previously. Animation as a form of storytelling is even less constricted by the laws of physics and the rules of our own reality. We can purposely break those rules to create a visually pleasing image. For that reason, animation holds a special place in my heart.

Q. What non-CG artwork inspires you?

A. I'm passionate about traditional fine arts as well as photography, and especially the subject of light. When I'm not lighting animated movies, I am trying to capture the light through other means, such as using a paintbrush or a camera lens.

I love French Impressionism and the American Hudson Valley school of painting. There is something primal that speaks to me when I see an awe-inspiring landscape painted in vivid colors that managed to masterfully capture the light.

Q. When first starting your master light rig, what is your approach? Do you light right away? Do you look at reference? Do you do paintovers?

A. This tends to vary by sequence and project. For more familiar lighting scenarios that I have done many times in the past, I would probably dive right in and start pushing lights around.

For more complex lighting scenarios that maybe I have not done extensively before, I would most certainly look at reference. Google Images search is an amazing resource for just about anything.

I would start with any artwork that is provided by the design department in the form of paintings and color keys, gather supporting photographic reference, and start wrapping my mind around it all. For me, lighting is a like playing in a sandbox.

I may have an idea where I'm going when I start, but being a very visual person I have to see it to know if it's working or not. It's a process of making adjustments and refinements through which the image kinda takes a life of its own. It tells me where it wants to go, and I'm just there to give it a push.

Q. How does your approach change between master lighting a shot versus lighting an individual shot?

A. The basic approach is similar, although when lighting a master shot I am very conscious of the fact that someone else will need to work with my lighting rig and use it as a starting point, and therefore I try to keep the setup as clean and organized as possible. When I'm just doing a one-off shot by myself that no one else needs to touch, things tend to be somewhat looser, and probably not quite as tidy. I'm definitely not the type that keeps stuff on their desk aligned at perfect 90 degree angles.

Q. What do you think is lighting's largest contribution to an animated film?

A. Hah! Ask a lighting person a question like that, and of course you will get the following answer. Lighting is a crucial part of filmmaking. Our lights guide the eye of a viewer and bring order to chaos. They set the mood and enhance the emotional beats of the story. Without lighting, you have nothing. OK, well … you may have "something," but it will not be as interesting!

Q. Where do you think the future of lighting is headed?

A. We are heading pretty fast towards real time technology, and it's a very exciting time to be a lighter. A day will come soon when "rendering" as we know it today will be a concept that will pass into history books, much like VCR tapes and phones with rotary dials. We will have full-blown global illumination with all the bells and whistles, and adjustments will be instantaneous. It would be a mistake, though, to think that this change will spell the end of lighting artist as a profession, just because software and hardware will be sophisticated enough to automatically do the grunt work that we do now. The "Make Pretty" button does not exist now, nor will it ever, because beauty is a highly subjective concept that cannot be replicated by a machine.

Computers are still just a tool, and there will still be a need for an artistic eye to shape the look and feel of sets through lighting, to make the characters look appealing and to balance all of the elements together.

Q. If you could tell yourself one piece of advice when you were first starting out in this industry, what would it be?

A. Work hard, and don't let your spirits get dampened by the naysayers. There will be plenty of people who will tell you that it will be hard or even impossible to get a job when you are first starting out. The industry is small and competitive, but if you really want to be part of it, you can make it happen. There will be ups and downs, and your journey may take you where you never thought it would, but understand that you can have a fulfilling career even if you are not working for one of the "big" studios. As long as you are happy doing what you love, that's all that matters.

Q. In your opinion, what makes a good lighting artist?

A. Understanding how to use the light and shadow to manipulate value, create contrast, and to use that contrast to your advantage. Understanding how colors relate to one another, and how to make them play with or against each other. Color theory is important, and a lighting artist that uses it well will be able to create a more successful image.

Interview
with Kurt Kaminski

Lighter :: Walt Disney Animation Studios.

Q. What is your current job/role at your company?
A. I'm currently a Lighter at Walt Disney Animation Studios and previously a Lead Lighter at DreamWorks Animation.

Q. What inspired you to become an artist on CG films?
A. I've always been attracted to the freedom that comes with making something from scratch. Cartoons and animated films allow for visual and narrative ideas to flow uninhibited by the laws of nature, and in that way are kind of a direct connection to the imagination. Computer graphics gives us a huge array of tools to play with these ideas at a high level. Of course, seeing this stuff in action had the biggest impact on me as a kid. Films like *Who Framed Roger Rabbit?*, *Jurassic Park*, and *The Nightmare Before Christmas* gave me an itch that I didn't know how to scratch until I started pursuing computer graphics.

Q. What non-CG artwork inspires you?
A. There's just so much out there. I like art that helps us see things in larger or totally unique contexts that we would otherwise be oblivious to. Edward Burtynsky and Ernst Haeckel come to mind, as well as what David Wilson has done in the Museum of Jurassic Technology. Some of the art stemming from the sciences is really amazing as well. I'm a huge fan of Michael Hansmeyer and Henry Segerman. Nature is the ultimate inspiration.

Q. When first starting your master light rig, what is your approach? Do you light right away? Do you look at reference? Do you do paintovers?

A. My approach to lighting anything is "broad strokes," so finding the things that are contributing the most to the look is the first order of business. What is actually happening in the sequence? From there, depending on the complexity, I might start lighting right away (a sunny exterior, for example), or I'll gather information via paintovers, photo reference, and other films. At the same time I'll begin considering the unique challenges each sequence comes with, such as heavy effects or computationally expensive set pieces. At some point images start happening, more information is collected, and the process is underway. The manner in which the rig actually comes together is different for every sequence. I learn something new every time.

Q. How does your approach change between master lighting a shot versus lighting an individual shot?

A. The approach stays the same—broad strokes. Getting the main ideas and biggest contributing factors down first still applies to individual shots as much as it does to developing the rig, it's just that your brush strokes will get smaller and more precise until the shot is finaled. The biggest practical difference with individual shots is the shift in focus to character lighting. The environment will usually be pretty well established by the rig, so now it's all about getting the characters to look good.

Q. What do you think is lighting's largest contribution to an animated film?

A. We are hardwired to understand lighting phenomena, so when we see it in an animated film it helps to draw the viewer in, adding belief and gravity to the story. The result is lighting's biggest contribution—making it look amazing.

Q. Where do you think the future of lighting is headed?

A. Technologically, lighting has been on a path towards ever more physically accurate models, even in animated films. The current trend in adopting stochastic raytracers demands that lighters have an increasingly intimate understanding of how light behaves in the real world. Beyond that, I expect greater integration with compositing and further crossover with video games as their tools rapidly become more filmic. Virtual reality is also an interesting prospect and presents a bunch of new aesthetic challenges for the next generation of lighters.

Q. If you could tell yourself one piece of advice when you were first starting out in this industry what would it be?

A. Broad strokes!

Q. In your opinion, what makes a good lighting artist?

A. Someone who is both a great photographer and a fearless problem solver will almost certainly be an excellent lighting artist.

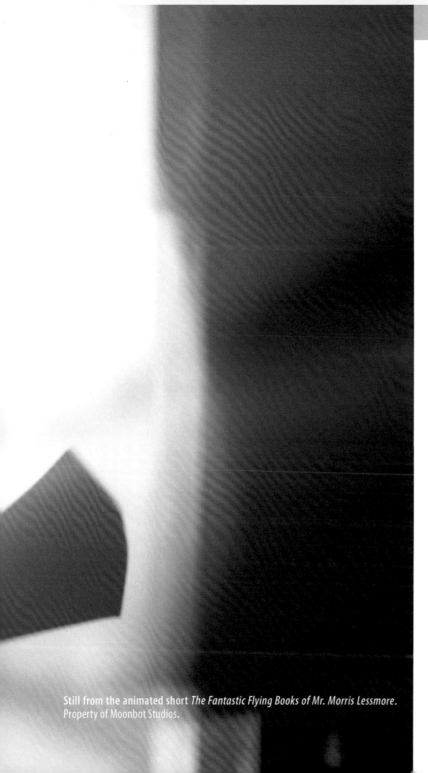

11

Closing Statements

Having a successful career as a lighting artist takes more than just the technical and artistic abilities already discussed in the book. Like any career, there are the ins and outs of the logistics of the industry that must be taken into consideration. Just as there is no magic button for lighting a shot, there is no single answer to how to become a successful artist in the industry. There are many elements that should be considered when beginning a career and continue to be focused on when moving forward. The common question is: What are the keys to landing the first job and how does one become successful once in that job? This chapter will explore these more human elements that go with getting your first job and being successful in this industry.

Getting Started as a Lighting Artist

Getting a first job in this industry can be a daunting, stressful, and difficult process. It can try the patience and shake the confidence of even the most talented artists. This is an exceptionally difficult time, but artists can take comfort in knowing that anyone who has ever been successful in this industry started out in the exact same situation.

Demo Reel

The demo reel is the most important weapon an artist has when hunting for a first job. In short, a demo reel is a one- to three-minute video compilation of an artist's best work. An education and degrees are great, but if an artist cannot demonstrate the ability to translate that knowledge into beautiful images then it does not matter. Recruiters and companies need the artist to demonstrate the skills to do the tasks they will be paying him or her to complete.

The first thing anyone reviewing a demo reel will look for is the ability to demonstrate the core, aesthetic concepts of being a lighter. Does the artist understand how to create mood and influence the story through lighting? Does the artist know how to balance light and color to make an aesthetically pleasing final image? The ability to do this repeatedly in multiple lighting circumstances is exactly what a feature animation house is looking for.

Generally speaking, the software or renderer used in creating the work for the demo reel is secondary. Many animation studios have some form of proprietary pipeline or renderer and know they will need to train any incoming artist on this. What they cannot train is the artist's eye and ability to take that technical knowledge and turn it into a beautiful image. By demonstrating these abilities, the artist can visually demonstrate that he or she is ready to tackle the challenges of the job.

Less is More

It is often said that a demo reel is only as strong as its weakest element. That is because a demo reel is regarded as a collection of the best work created by that artist. It is meant to exemplify the artistic ability and aesthetic judgment of that artist. If one piece of the demo reel is below par compared with the other work being displayed it will be perceived that the artist may not have the aesthetic aptitude to distinguish that work from others.

This means the artist must make difficult decisions. Often artists have too many emotional connections to work that can thwart their judgment. Maybe a specific shot took months to complete and the artist could never imagine editing it out after working on it for so long. Or a shot is about the artist's relationship with a loved one and therefore carries extra weight even though the visuals are weak. In these situations artists would be wise to seek the advice of others whose opinions they trust. They should ask several people what piece is the strongest and which is the weakest, then listen carefully to the responses and take action if the opinion is in general agreement.

Smart edits are extremely important to the construction of a successful demo reel. Be sure that the strongest work is in the beginning. Many times reviewers will never reach the end of the reel if the first few images do not pique their interest. As an artist, you need to engage the reviewers immediately, otherwise you may lose the reviewers' attention before they can review your best work. This is why it is important to put your best work first.

Cater the Demo Reel for the Job

The person reviewing the reel is trying to decide if his or her company should invest a large amount of money into a particular artist to complete a specific task. The specific task will vary depending on the studio. Some studios will require more compositing while others will require shading work. Some studios will want to see more photorealistic environmental renderings while some studios are more stylized and focus heavily on character lighting.

So, as an artist, give them what they want. Demonstrate the skills they are looking for and prove their money will be spent wisely by hiring you. Do not waste their time with a bunch of work that doesn't apply to the job. If the company is about creating animated features with strong character lighting, they will overlook a shot that proves an artist can integrate a cell phone into an abstract background. It is up to you, as the submitting artist, to cater the reel to convince the reviewer that you are able to complete the task.

Including Photography and Other Traditional Artwork

This topic is difficult and opinions tend to vary widely. While photographs, paintings, sketches, or other traditional artwork can distinguish the artistic skill of one artist versus another, they should only be used if the work is exceptional. It cannot be stressed enough that the work demonstrated on the reel must directly relate to the job in question. The demo reel should be the artist's absolute best work that is applicable to the job. Only if the traditional artwork falls into this category should it be included and only at the very end of the reel.

Demo Reel Integrity

This should go without saying, but artists should never, ever falsify information on a demo reel. They should not add work that is not theirs and they should never claim to have done more on a shot than they did. This can be the fastest way to not only lose out on one job opportunity, but also completely ruin a career.

Even though this seems obvious, there are countless occurrences when this has taken place. Reviewers have even encountered instances where they see their own work on an applicant's reel. What do you think that applicant's chances are of landing that job? Worse yet, after it is revealed that the applicant lied on his or her demo reel, what are the chances that artist will get hired at that company ever again? This industry is incredibly small and word of these types of events spread quickly. The end result is that an artist's reputation acquires a huge blemish that may never go away.

Connections

Connections are such a powerful tool when job hunting. Reaching out to former co-workers, college classmates, and acquaintances can be an amazing way to find out about employment opportunities. Connections can inform artists of jobs before they are even posted. Jobs are frequently obtained through connections as opposed to just submitting a demo reel and resumé because these submissions can be accompanied with a good word from someone already at the studio.

For those reading this that are still in school, these connections are already being formed. The work ethic and reliability displayed even at this point can influence landing a job several years down the road. Recruiters will often asked current employees that went to school with a candidate what their impressions of that person were. Was the candidate a positive person who was easy to work with? On group projects, did the candidate contribute a fair share and prove to be a good team member? There are instances where a person's behavior when in school will jeopardize the opportunity at a job several years later.

Applying for Jobs

Early on in an artist's career it can be difficult to determine which job openings are realistic opportunities. The opportunities at the top feature animation studios could be the main focus of recent graduates, but often the major studios will not even consider someone without industry experience. The best bet for students and young artists is to focus either on entry-level artistic or technical positions within those companies or on jobs at smaller houses.

Smaller companies are actually a great way to go for artists early in their careers because of the opportunities they provide. These companies are often working on shorter projects like commercials or television shows. These shorter deadlines mean artists get to work on many projects and quickly expand both their knowledge and their demo reels. Larger companies can take a year or more between projects and this makes it difficult for artists to prove their worth and grow quickly. Smaller studios also give artists the opportunity to spread their wings and have a hand in a larger part of the pipeline, while the larger companies will make artists specialize. Also, the shorter turnarounds at commercial houses can lead to more frequent job openings while the larger houses can go years without lighting positions becoming available.

Managing an Online Profile

One of the first things some companies do when interested in a person is to complete an online search. This will lead to social media accounts, projects the artist worked on, personal websites, and any other information that is readily available about the artist online. This is an inevitable truth so it is best for the artist to ensure that his or her online persona is not a liability.

There are the obvious elements that exist online that anyone applying for a job would be wise to remove. A good rule of thumb is to try and remove anything compromising that you wouldn't want your mother to see. Anything that depicts the artist doing anything illegal should be removed, or anything that shows general immaturity.

Should artists remove all photos of parties and having fun? Absolutely not. It is actually a good thing to show that an individual has a bit of a personality and has interests outside of work. This industry is very relaxed, but the competition for positions can be tight and even a small implication of bad decision making can be the breaking point between getting a job and not.

Negativity can actually hurt a candidate more than anything. If the online search reveals someone that complains a lot and is generally a negative person, that could be a big red flag to a manager. Remember, the employer is wondering if an individual is someone he or she wants to spend eight to fourteen hours a day with, five to seven days a week. If that person spends hours every day complaining, then it is an issue. The worst situation is if the online profile shows the candidate complaining about a previous job and boss, because chances are he or she will do the same again. So be aware of the online representation of yourself and make sure it is not making it harder to get a job.

Interviewing

The key for any artist interviewing for a position is to be prepared and confident in one's abilities. Being prepared starts with researching the company. Discover the history of the company, especially the projects they have done and the current projects they are working on. Nothing is worse than going into an interview at one company and praising the work done on a commercial or film when it was actually created by a rival.

Other preparations prior to the interview include:

- Make sure to know where the interview is being held and how long it takes to get there. Tardiness makes for a terrible first impression.
- Wear something professional that is comfortable. The goal is to be presentable while still being loose and relaxed. This industry is very informal so something clean and casual is perfectly fine.
- Prepare questions for the interviewer. Inevitably, he or she will ask if the interviewee has any questions and it is always a good sign when a candidate has questions queued up and ready to go.
- Practice answering questions in the mirror or with someone else. This practice will make the real thing much more manageable.

Displaying confidence can be a tricky thing because the artist must show pride in his or her own ability while maintaining a level of humility. Over-confidence can easily be read as arrogance and can be off-putting to the interviewer. The last thing the interviewer wants is to bring in someone who is a "know-it-all" and will be difficult to train. Finding a nice balance between the two will lead to a good interview.

One approach is to treat each interview like seeing an old friend for the first time in years. Treat the interviewer as if he or she is familiar and therefore comfortable and the interviewee is just having a chat to catch up on the last few years. This will make the candidate's greeting warmer and more sincere and the conversation more natural. When this is working at its best, the interviewee will take the lead of the interviewer and reciprocate the warmth.

After the interview is complete, make sure to follow up with a thank you email or letter, something that shows appreciation for them to have taken time out of their busy day to conduct the interview. This is an old practice, but it is still appreciated.

It's Not You … It's Me

Something that often gets misunderstood by those first entering the industry is that so much of landing a job comes down to timing. There are instances in which it doesn't matter how great the demo reel was or how well the interview went, other external forces determine whether or not a candidate will get the job. An artist could be charming and talented and exactly what a company is looking for, but sometimes there are extenuating circumstances.

One is the availability of the position. There have been times when a candidate has interviewed for a position and everyone agreed he or she would be a good fit for the role. Then something happens and the money that was delegated to hiring that position needs to be reapplied elsewhere and the company can no longer afford to hire anyone new. So even though the interview was great and the department loved the candidate, there was no longer a position available.

Another situation is when a position has already been offered to one artist, but the company continues to hold interviews in case that initial artist turns it down. So it doesn't matter how great those other interviews are, if the person who was first offered the job accepts, no one in those additional interviews will get the job. This does not mean the artist should not try because a good interview could open opportunities in the future. If the candidate makes a good impression, the employer will most definitely remember that person for future employment opportunities. Regarding the immediate position, there was nothing that could have been done to receive that job offer so, sometimes, it is an "It's not you, it's me" scenario.

Salary Negotiation

The first job offer has come in. Congratulations! Now is the time to start the salary negotiations. Salary negotiations are absolutely an art and each situation is unique. There is only so much the artist can control so it is important to focus on what is manageable during a salary negotiation.

The starting point for salary negotiation is to understand who has the leverage. Unfortunately, when it is the first job, the company normally has almost all the leverage unless the candidate has multiple offers. They know there are many young artists that want a particular position and can therefore find the one that will accept the salary they are willing to pay. In other circumstances later in an artist's career, when one company is trying to hire artists away from another company, then the artist will have more leverage and room for negotiation. In either case, it is important to understand the dynamics of the situation so the negotiation can be managed successfully.

The other main area of focus is for the artist to realistically assess what amount of money he or she will be willing to take to accept the position. There are multiple factors at play including cost of living for the given area. It is much more costly to live in Los Angeles, London, or New York City versus other cities. Does the company cover other expenses like health insurance, retirement savings, and/or paying to move the artist? Does the company offer overtime or a bonus based on the success of projects? All of this will play a role in the negotiation process and determining how much an artist will need to live in a certain location.

Thriving in the Industry

The treacherous waters of finding a job have been navigated and now it is time to start the new career. Obviously, the most important thing is to show up and do the job as proficiently and as well as can be done. There are, however, some other bits of advice that have been learned over the years that could definitely benefit those just starting out.

First Impressions Stick

The first few weeks at a new job are of the utmost importance for establishing a baseline for long-term success at a company. These are the days when a new worker will meet and possibly complete his or her first assignment with supervisors and co-workers. How a new employee behaves and performs during this time period will create an identity that could stick for a number of years. Is this person an employee that comes in on time and delivers the assignment ahead of schedule? Or is this someone that says something is going to be done and then takes a week longer than expected to finish it? Is he or she polite, hard-working, and extremely grateful to be working in that environment? Or does he or she complain often and seem hard to work with? These first impressions greatly matter so it is best to be aware of how you are displaying yourself to the new co-workers.

Be Humble and Be Grateful for Others' Time

Confidence is a great thing, but when first starting a job it is best to err on the side of humility. Understand that the artists already at the company have probably been doing this for a number of years and have a great deal of experience. While a new hire's own experiences and past work are extremely valuable and could benefit the new company, when first starting out it is better to listen, learn, and focus on becoming familiar with the new environment.

For the first few weeks at a new job, new hires should have a notepad glued to one hand and a pen to the other. They should listen intently to everything said and jot down notes as they go. Even if the note is using some in-house jargon that is not yet understood, still write it down and figure it out later. This practice will benefit new hires in a number of ways:

- It will make it visibly clear to those conducting the training that they are listening and retaining the information.
- After the demonstration, new hires will often have questions about sections that were covered in the demonstration. They can refer back to the notes instead of asking the person to re-explain something that has already been covered. Nothing annoys a busy person more than having to explain something multiple times to the same person.
- By not asking obvious questions, new hires can appear as though they are intelligent people that only need to be told something once—a skill highly sought by any supervisor.

Be Fast

The first thing any artist wants to do is come into a studio and prove he or she can make beautiful images. This is clearly important and definitely something worth striving for. The one element that gets overlooked that is probably more important is speed. The easiest way to impress supervisors is to complete assignments quickly. This is because new artists are often given the lower priority shots and ones with a lesser difficulty. While the temptation may be there to spend countless hours tweaking and perfecting every pixel of these shots, it is often most important to get a solid image rendered out quickly and available for review and approval. This isn't to say that the artist should make aesthetically poor images. It is just far more important to have three good-looking shots ready for review rather than one great one.

Be Someone You Would Want to Work With

The easiest way to describe how to behave when first getting a job is to visualize the ideal co-worker and then be that person. The first step is just to be a positive member of the team. Do not sit around complaining to everyone or whining about the task at hand. Does this mean everyone needs to have bubbly, upbeat personalities? Absolutely not. Be yourself and just focus on the positives, and always maintain the attitude that you are going to get things done.

Be Reliable

When you say you are going to get something done by a specific time, get it done. The last thing co-workers want to hear is a bunch of excuses, so figure out a way to get it done. A great way to get on your co-workers' good side is to be someone that can be counted on to deliver.

One facet of delivering work on time is managing expectations. When first starting it is common to want to give the most optimis-

tic answer to the question of "When is that assignment going to be completed?" If you are working on something that will probably take two days there is the temptation to say it will only take one, to have others be impressed with your efficiency. The problem is when something goes wrong, as it always seems to, then the assignment will still take two days to complete. Now the assignment is late and everyone is disappointed. Conversely, imagine if you had set the expectations lower by saying that there may be some issues and the task could take upwards of three days. Then you still deliver it in two days and everyone is happy because you delivered the assignment early. It is the exact same outcome, but in one situation everyone is happy with you, while in the other they are disappointed.

Always Hit the Notes

There are times when an artist will disagree with the notes given by the director or supervisor. Lighting is subjective and this will definitely happen on occasion. There may be a temptation to demonstrate artistic prowess and ignore this note and do it another way. This is the worst thing new artists can do if they would like to have a chance at getting their idea in the final product. No matter how good it looks, the supervisor's first thought will be, "This is not what I asked for."

The thing to do is to hit their note exactly. Then do a secondary version of the same shot with the look the artist envisioned. This can be done through lighting, but it could be equally effective through a quick mockup in the composite or even just a single frame still. This will do a few things:

1. It will show the director or supervisor the respect they deserve. They probably have a lot of experience in the industry and ascended to the position they occupy by having a good eye that should be trusted. Put yourself in their shoes. You would want your notes to be hit, too.
2. The two versions can quickly be compared and the director or supervisor can quickly make a decision based on two visuals instead of theoretical ideas.
3. Even if the alternative look the artist has created is not chosen, this shows initiative and the fact that the artist tried to push the envelope and did it in a respectful and professional manner.

Email Etiquette

In most companies, much of the work and communication is done via email. These emails can be tricky and require a certain etiquette. To start, stick with these simple rules until the email culture of a certain company is determined:

- Keep emails short and concise. People are extremely busy and receive a lot of email. If the main purpose of the email is buried in the second paragraph, it will get overlooked. Try and limit emails to just a few sentences.
- If someone sends an email requesting that an artist do something, always respond as quickly as possible that the email has been received and the task has begun. Even a simple response of "On it" works perfectly fine. If no response is received, the sender may think the email was missed and become frustrated even if the work is being done. This is just good communication.

- Avoid sarcasm until a higher level of comfort is obtained with co-workers. Sarcasm or any humor that requires a tone of voice can be completely lost in an email and the sender can be misinterpreted as being rude or impolite. At first it is best to avoid those problems altogether until a stronger reputation is established.
- Limit emoticons and exclamation points. Although they are perfectly acceptable for some, others view these as unprofessional and childish.
- Do not send email links to funny articles or video clips. Again, a new hire is trying to make the impression of being a focused, hard worker and these types of email give the impression of someone slacking on the job. Other people may send these types of links, but until new hires are established it would be wise to avoid them.
- Finish the email thread. If an email thread is reviewed after it is completed there should always be one final email with a simple "Thanks" or "My pleasure" that shows all participants that the conversation is done.

Learn the Office Rules

Every office has special rules that all employees must follow. These rules are unique to specific offices and can be the source of much frustration from veteran employees if the new people don't adhere to them. The rules are usually like:

- If someone finishes the coffee, make a fresh pot.
- Don't eat other people's food from the common refrigerator.
- Make sure to put the proper recyclables in the proper bins.
- Maintain a respectable volume.

These things may seem inconsequential, but they could be a huge source of irritation for co-workers.

Recommendations

The same way you will reach out to your connections when job hunting, others will reach out to you once you have established your career. In fact, the situation will often arise when a company is looking for new hires and will turn to existing employees for recommendations. Recommendations are not something to be taken lightly. We all have friends looking for jobs who we would love to help out, but are you willing to stake your reputation on the line for that individual? Take a minute to think this over and be realistic. If that individual comes in and performs poorly, the disappointment and negative burden will be placed just as much on you as on him or her. Only give official recommendations when you are absolutely certain that person will perform admirably.

Final Thoughts

In many ways, this is a unique and rewarding career path. We get to make pretty pictures all day long and generally entertain people with our work. We are able to satisfy the artistic side of our brains while simultaneously tackling technical issues. Some of these images will last a lifetime and will always be a source of pride. We hope you will join this industry and help make the world more beautiful, one frame at a time!

Interview with Deb Stone

Manager of Recruiting and Talent Development :: Blue Sky Studios.

Q. What is your current job/role at your company?
A. I am the Manager of Recruiting and Talent Development at Blue Sky Studios.

Q. What inspired you to work in the CG industry?
A. I was lucky and actually fell into this industry but have been inspired to stay in it ever since. I have worked for two major studios in this industry and there is one thing that has never wavered: it's the people that make this industry what it is; they are passionate and excited about the work they do and it keeps me inspired to be around them every day.

Q. You have seen countless students' reels. What is something that makes one student reel stand out from the rest?
A. It is a challenge for students to make their reels stand out these days. The reels that do stand out show tests related to the specific discipline they are applying for and each test in the reel is artistically and technically sound. We need to see that the person really has an understanding for their craft. It's the reels that think outside the box showcasing personal tests or shots from a short that go above and beyond a standard classroom test. I'm constantly telling students to show only their best work. The worst thing in a reel will hurt their reel the most.

Q. When speaking with potential candidates about a position, what are you looking for? Positive attitude? Good communication skills? Clear knowledge of the subject matter?

A. First and foremost, for most disciplines a strong reel is the most important thing. Once a candidate makes it to a phone or in-person interview, they need to have a positive attitude, good communication skills, and knowledge of their craft. Depending on how technical the position is there could be a lot of detailed questions that a person will need to be prepared to answer. It's also always important that we can tell from an interview that the person will be a good team player and that they are humble and eager to learn.

Q. What advice would you give someone going into an interview? How can they put their best foot forward?

A. I think there are three things a candidate can do to prep for an interview.

1. I know it's hard, but try not to be nervous; try to be yourself. Sometimes nerves can get the best of someone, which makes it hard for the interviewer to really get a feel for who the candidate really is.
2. Prepare yourself for the interview, do some research on the company, make sure you know about the history of the company and why you as a candidate are interested in that company.
3. Enthusiasm and humility go a long way!

Q. What is the worst thing someone could do in an interview?

A. The worst thing someone could do is lie. It is important that the candidate can explain everything in their reel and on their resumé. For example, if a candidate says they are knowledgeable about a specific tool, that candidate had better be able to clearly articulate their understanding and explain how they have used that tool in the past. As a candidate you never want to get a question in an interview that you can't answer, especially if you say you are knowledgeable about that topic on your resumé.

Q. What should someone include and exclude in their reel?

A. A reel should contain only the person's best work. There is no right or wrong answer on how long a reel should be, but for students a reel should only be a few tests or projects. Reels should also start with the candidate's strongest piece and contain only their best work! (Am I sounding like a broken record yet?)

When applying to a company, candidates should tailor their reels for that company. For example, feature animation studios (for the most part) want to see people who are more specialized in a skill set where smaller studios may want to see people who are generalists.

There is also a difference in styles between features, TV, and games. It's OK to create multiple reels; just make sure when applying to a company that you know what they are looking for.

Q. In your opinion, what makes a good lighting artist?
A. A good lighting artist has a good artistic eye and can make their shot look like a piece of art. They understand how to frame their characters and how to play with highlights, shadows, and ambience in a way that makes the viewer intrigued to keep watching. The lighting in a shot should guide the viewer's eye to the action and should not be distracting.

Q. If you could tell yourself one piece of advice when you were first starting out in this industry, what would it be?
A. The industry is really small, so get to know as many people as you can and build your network. You never know when your connections and networks will help you land your next job, so always be nice! You don't want to tarnish your reputation by being a jerk.

Index